T0323614

Governing the Reformed University

Universities are important public institutions and are seen as key drivers for a country's economic and intellectual development. Their ability to deliver relevant research and education at the highest level have an impact on growth and progress in society, and governments attempt to control and govern the development of the universities. It is no longer left to the individual researcher or the institution to determine the role of the university.

Universities have traditionally had a special role in society with a high degree of autonomy and independence. They have been described as a self-governing Republic of Science and their internal organization is characterized as "academic tribes". However, universities can also be viewed as institutions with somewhat similar characteristics as other public institutions with highly professionalized staff.

Governing the Reformed University is a coherent volume based on a unique data set. The aim of the book is to quantitatively and qualitatively understand and explain how reforms and management instruments are implemented and how it influences different levels of the organization from the top management level to the employees within universities. It contributes to the knowledge of reform and reform impact in higher education. It also adds to our understanding of management and governance at universities and through which mechanisms management works at universities.

This book builds on and adds to the knowledge of studies of reform and governance at universities. The data used in the book consist of a number of data sets and is collected as part of a comprehensive research project. Academics and policy makers alike in the fields of public administration, public management, public policy, educational studies, and accountancy will find this of high interest.

Dr. Niels Ejersbo is Vice-director at University College Copenhagen, Denmark.

Dr. Carsten Greve is Professor at Department of Business and Politics at Copenhagen Business School, Denmark.

Dr. Signe Pihl-Thingvad is Associate Professor at Department of Political Science and Public Management, University of Southern Denmark, Denmark.

Routledge Critical Studies in Public Management
Series editor: Stephen Osborne

The study and practice of public management has undergone profound changes across the world. Over the last quarter century, we have seen

- increasing criticism of public administration as the over-arching framework for the provision of public services,
- the rise (and critical appraisal) of the Mew Public Management as an emergent paradigm for the provision of public services,
- the transformation of the "public sector" into the cross-sectoral provision of public services, and
- the growth of the governance of inter-organizational relationship as an essential element in the provision of public services.

In reality these trends have not so much replaced each other as elided or co-existed together—the public policy processes has not gone away as a legitimate topic of study, intra-organizational management continue to be essential to the efficient provision of public services, whilst the governance of inter-organizational and inter-sectoral relationships is now essential to the effective provision of these services.

Further, whilst the study of public management has been enriched by the contribution of a range of insights from the "mainstream" management literature it has also contributed to this literature in such areas as networks and inter-organizational collaboration, innovation, and stakeholder theory.

This series is dedicated to presenting and critiquing this important body of theory and empirical study. It will publish books that both explore and evaluate the emergent and developing nature of public administration, management and governance (in theory and practice) and examine the relationship with and contribution to the over-arching disciplines of management and organizational sociology.

Books in the series will be of interest to academics and researchers in this field, students undertaking advanced studies of it as part of their undergraduate or postgraduate degree and reflective policy makers and practitioners.

Collaborative Governance for Local Economic Development
Lessons from Countries around the World
Edited by Denita Cepiku, So Hee Jeon, and David K. Jesuit

Governing the Reformed University
Edited by Niels Ejersbo, Carsten Greve, and Signe Pihl-Thingvad

For more information about this series, please visit: www.routledge.com/ Routledge-Critical-Studies-in-Public-Management/book-series/RSPM

Governing the Reformed University

Edited by Niels Ejersbo,
Carsten Greve, and
Signe Pihl-Thingvad

Routledge
Taylor & Francis Group

NEW YORK AND LONDON

First published 2020
by Routledge
605 Third Avenue, New York, NY 10017

and by Routledge
2 Park Square, Milton Park, Abingdon, Oxon, OX14 4RN

First issued in paperback 2021

Routledge is an imprint of the Taylor & Francis Group, an informa business

Publisher's Note
The publisher has gone to great lengths to ensure the quality of this
reprint but points out that some imperfections in the original copies
may be apparent.

Library of Congress Cataloging-in-Publication Data
A catalog record for this book has been requested

ISBN 13: 978-1-03-208358-2 (pbk)
ISBN 13: 978-1-138-06842-1 (hbk)

Typeset in Sabon
by Apex CoVantage, LLC

Contents

Preface   vii
List of Contributors   ix

1 Introduction   1
   NIELS EJERSBO, CARSTEN GREVE, AND
   SIGNE PIHL-THINGVAD

2 Data and Methods   18
   NIELS EJERSBO, PERNILLE BAK PEDERSEN, AND
   SIGNE PIHL-THINGVAD

3 University Reforms in Context—The Relationship
   Between University Reforms and General Reforms
   in the Public Sector   27
   CARSTEN GREVE AND NIELS EJERSBO

4 Controlling Autonomy: Governmental Regulation
   of Danish Universities From 1989 to 2015   40
   PERNILLE BAK PEDERSEN

5 Board Influence and Interaction With University
   Management   67
   NIELS EJERSBO AND CARSTEN GREVE

6 Department Chairs—Modern Managers or Old
   Administrators?   81
   NIELS EJERSBO AND CARSTEN GREVE

7 Autonomy and Performance Contracts at Universities   98
   NIELS EJERSBO, SIGNE PIHL-THINGVAD, AND
   MAIKEN K. WESTERGAARD

8 Academics and Performance Systems 118
POUL ERIK MOURITZEN AND NIELS OPSTRUP

9 Modern Management and Working Conditions
in Academia 140
SIGNE PIHL-THINGVAD AND NIELS OPSTRUP

10 Conclusion 158
NIELS EJERSBO, CARSTEN GREVE, AND
SIGNE PIHL-THINGVAD

Index 166

Preface

Universities are important public institutions and are seen as key drivers for a country's economic and intellectual development). Their ability to deliver relevant research and education at the highest level have an impact on growth and progress in society, and governments attempt to control and govern the development of the universities. It is no longer left to the individual researcher or the institution to determine the role of the university. Universities across the world have been through comprehensive reforms during the past decades). Many of the university reforms have followed reform trends in other areas of the public sector with emphasis on competition, performance management, arm-length steering, and professionalization of management.

This book is about university reforms, how these reforms correspond with general reform trends in the public sector, the reaction to reforms at different managerial levels at the university, and how governance instruments influence the academic environment and work environment.

It is a coherent volume based on a unique data set. The aim of the book is to quantitatively and qualitatively understand and explain how reforms and management instruments are implemented and how it influences different levels of the organization from the top management level to the employees. It contributes to the knowledge of reform and reform impact in higher education. It also adds to our understanding of management and governance at universities and through which mechanisms management works at universities. The book offers insights relevant for understanding reform and governance at other highly professionalized and knowledge intensive public institutions.

The book draws on data connected in relation to the research project "Governing, Funding and Performance of Universities". The project was headed by Professor Poul Erik Mouritzen. We are grateful to all the members of the project for contributing to the data collection, commenting on the idea for this book and contributing with chapters. Members of the project's international advisory board, Professors Margit Osterloh, Barry Bozeman, Ivar Bleiklie, Bruno S. Frey and Poul Wouters gave valuable input to the research project.

Finally, we thank The Velux Foundation for supporting the project.

Odense, Denmark   Niels Ejersbo
Copenhagen, Denmark   Carsten Greve
Odense, Denmark   Signe Pihl-Thingvad

Contributors

Dr. Niels Ejersbo, Vice-director at University College Copenhagen, Denmark.

Dr. Carsten Greve, Professor at Department of Business and Politics, Copenhagen Business School, Denmark.

Dr. Poul Erik Mouritzen, Professor at Department of Political Science, Aarhus University.

Dr. Niels Opstrup, Associate Professor at Department of Political Science and Public Management, University of Southern Denmark.

Pernille Bak Pedersen, Consultant, Aarhus University.

Dr. Signe Pihl-Thingvad, Associate Professor at Department of Political Science and Public Management, University of Southern Denmark.

Maiken Westergaard, Consultant at Odense Municipality.

1 Introduction

*Niels Ejersbo, Carsten Greve, and
Signe Pihl-Thingvad*

Universities have experienced massive reforms during the past couple of decades (Bleiklie & Lepori 2017). Universities have undergone a process to become more managerial than governed by professionals or being part of a traditional hierarchy. Universities strive to become "complete" organizations, but there are still many elements that prohibit that move (Seeber et al. 2015). Universities have recently been characterized as "penetrated hierarchies" that are influenced by external pressures for control in the internal organization (Bleiklie, Enders & Lepori 2015). Today, universities have moved away from the traditional "Humboldt model" towards "the enterprise university" (Marginson & Considine 2000), which does focus on knowledge discovery, but which is also preoccupied with performance measurement and management, competing for funding and students, and making strategic alliances to get ahead in global ranking systems. The development in universities is heavily influenced by "the rise of relevance" where universities are but one category of knowledge providers to governments and businesses (Bleiklie 2018). As Brookings scholar Darrell West (2016) has shown, organizations find themselves in an age of "megachange" with economic disruption, political upheaval, and social strife.

This book aims at answering key research questions related to university governance: (1) How are universities reformed and how do reforms influence universities as organizations? (2) How do governments control the autonomy of universities through government regulation? (3) How do universities cope with demands for improved performance management systems? (4) How are universities governed and managed after major university reforms? (5) How do faculty members react to performance management systems? (6) How does managerialism influence the working environment at the workplaces in universities?

By university governance we mean the institutions and processes, the structure, and the managerial practices in universities as part of the public sector. By managerialism we mean the use of management techniques and practices performed by appointed public managers in universities.

Our empirical material comes from a large study of universities in Denmark. A unique dataset has been created upon which we draw in our analyses in this book.

Reforms in the Public Sector and in Universities

Attempts to reform public institutions have been going on for several decades now, starting with the wave of New Public Management (NPM) reforms in the 1980s and 1990s. Reforms during the past decades are, compared to earlier reforms, treated as less a technical or legal matter and as less a national or sectoral matter (Pollitt & Bouckaert 2017). Now reform is viewed as an important political and economic matter that cuts across national and sector boundaries. Public management reforms take place across Europe, as a new study has shown (Hammerschmid, Van den Walle, Andrews & Bezes 2016), and in the Nordic countries (Greve, Lægreid & Rykkja 2016). The U.S. has a long history of making public management reforms where the research shows that reforms can be full of contradictions because of political disagreements that trickle down into government organizations (Radin 2012).

The literature on public management contains a large number of concepts and categorizations trying to capture the essence of reforms in the public sector. Established public governance paradigms include NPM (Hood 1991; Christensen & Lægreid 2011), New Public Governance and governance networks (Osborne 2010; Klijn & Koppenjan 2016), Digital Era Governance (Dunleavy, Margetts, Bastow & Tinkler 2006), Neo-Weberian State (Pollitt & Bouckaert 2017), and, most recently, public value management or governance (Bryson, Crosby & Bloomberg 2014). They are now well-known examples of concepts that emphasize different aspects of reforms in the public sector. NPM wanted to enhance the use of management styles from the private sector coupled with market mechanisms for public service delivery. NPM has been described by Dunleavy as "disaggregation + competition + incentivatization" (quoted in Pollitt & Bouckaert 2017). NPG focused more on the prolific evaluation of networks in public policy-making and implementation. Managers are here becoming network managers rather than public sector "CEOs" as in NPM. DEG put the spotlight on digitalization as a transformational and maybe even disruptive force in the public sector. Dunleavy and colleagues argued that as digital changes have transformed many sectors in the private sector (think of Amazon, Facebook and other social media, Airbnb), digital changes will also change the way the public sector works and relates to citizens. A Neo-Weberian State (NWS) is focused on keeping a commitment to bureaucrats and professionals in the public sector, but also recognizes that public services can be delivered more efficiently through better performance management and with greater attention to citizens' wishes. NWS is not totally "retro", but aims to couple efficient service delivery with a more responsible state, and thus keeping a distance to the more market-oriented approach of NPM. Finally, public value management and governance, as expressed by Mark Moore's seminal work on creating public value, and Bryson and colleagues' extension of that work to a focus on public value creation in governance networks, this latest attempt at the formulation of a public governance paradigm wants to underline the broad value creation responsibility that the public sector has.

Brunsson and Sahlin-Andersson (2000; Brunsson 2013) argue that public sector reforms can be interpreted at attempts at constructing organizations. Public organizations are "incomplete" in the sense that they lack some key characteristics of organizations. Reforms aim at incorporating key organization elements such as hierarchy, management, and rationality making public organizations look more like "real" organizations. "In many cases, the reforms were not aimed at the products of the public sector, at health care or education for example. Rather, they have represented attempts at changing the modes of managing, controlling and accounting for the actual production of such services" (ibid.: 722). Brunsson (2013: 66) followed up the approach in 2013 with this description:

> the central notion underlying most of the reforms was the idea and the ideal of the organization. The reforms constructed organizations, and modern organizations offer a perfect context for lofty ideas and ideals, making them highly reformist. The construction of organizations increases the likelihood of extensive and continued reforming.

Recent research on European universities has addressed this issue of becoming "complete organizations" and has found that universities have not reached that stage yet (Seeber et al. 2015).

If reforms are discussed in this organizational approach, universities become a very interesting case. Universities have traditionally been associated with a very high degree of autonomy both at the management level and among the researchers. Furthermore scholars argue that universities are internally fragmented because they consist of so many different professional groups with different interests, tasks, and institutional arrangements (Capano 2011: 1623; Christensen 2011; Kristensen, Nørreklit & Raffnsøe-Møller 2011; Kerr 1963). Therefore, in current research, universities are characterized by a high degree of both organizational and functional complexity, which make them more fluid and fragmented than "traditional organization". Furthermore, at universities, "Clients not only consume services but also have a voice in the decision-making process. Lines of authority are blurred and professional employees (i.e., professors) demand a high degree of autonomy for their work" (Sporn in Forest and Altbach 2007: 150). The traditional autonomy of universities are challenged and the state attempts to shape and control them more actively (Ferlie, Musselin & Andresani 2009: 2). Universities have traditionally been characterized as a self-governing Republic of Science (Polyanyi 1962) and their internal organization is characterized as "academic tribes" (Becher 1989), "loosely coupled systems" (Weick 1976), or "organized anarchies" (Cohen & March 1974). They have a high degree of both organizational and functional complexity, because they consist of so many different professional groups with different interests, tasks, and institutional arrangements that they are internally fragmented (Capano 2011: 1623; Christensen 2011; Kristensen et al. 2011; Kerr 1963). It might therefore be argued that universities differ from "traditional organizations" in most of their key elements.

Overall, the public sector reforms increases the need for political governance and strategic management of universities (Degn & Sørensen 2015: 932). Most recent university reforms may therefore be interpreted as a policy intention to professionalize the university management and organization (Degn & Sørensen 2012, 2015; Enders, de Boer & Weyer 2013: 7–8; Christensen 2011).

Reforms of universities especially target the internal organization of universities (Maassen, Larsen & Stensaker 2009) and try changing them into an instrument (Olsen 2007) in pursuit of efficiency, economic development, and, more broadly, public value creation (Moore 1995, 2013).

The attempt to transform universities into organizations fits with the NPM reform agenda which Brunsson (2013) also acknowledges. As stated earlier, NPM has primarily been about (1) using management inspiration from the private sector and focusing on efficient service delivery and improved performance, and (2) using market mechanisms in many different forms to put pressure on the university as an organization. This could be everything from extending user choice (viewing students as "customers") to making space for a new salary structure that rewards performance and attract top talent, including top managers.

We argue that three reform elements especially characterize university reform and have implications for how universities function, how they are organized, how they are managed, and how employees experience reforms. Most of them have some connection to the NPM reform agenda and the idea of the "enterprise university".

First, the organization of universities has been a prime target for the establishment of a more formal, coherent *and hierarchical organizational structure* within the university is a key element, and universities strive to become "complete" organizations in the phrase of Seeber et al. (2015).

Second and somewhat related, the reforms have put more emphasis on *managerialism understood as the role of professional management and leadership* and the formal role of rectors, deans, and department heads.

Third, universities must measure and account for their performance to a larger extent than earlier. As part of reforms, universities are obligated to implement different *performance management systems* and generally pay more attention to how well they perform on a number of different dimensions. In the Danish case, the university as an organization signs a performance contract with its principal, the government owner. Universities are also seen to be competing in a quasi-marketplace for funding, for students, and for attracting new academic personnel. Universities' performance is being measured in performance evaluations and international rankings.

It can be argued that these developments and reform elements reflect a general reform trend in the public sector and are as such not only a university phenomenon. The analysis of the international reform movement will confirm that public management reform has been occurring across almost all of the public sectors during the last three decades (Hammerschmid et al. 2016; Pollitt & Bouckaert 2017). In this book we will examine how these steps towards making universities "complete organizations" have consequences for and impact on the different organizational levels at the universities—from the top management to the academic employee. Theses consequences might be relevant for a broader description of what happens when reforms are implemented in public organizations in general. We will return to this point in our concluding chapter.

In the following section, we will comment on these three reform elements and show how they are reflected in the literature on higher education.

Formalizing Organization Structures and Establishment of Internal Hierarchy

The formalization of universities into more "normal" public sector organizations alongside hospitals, schools, police force, etc. has occurred over a long period. The challenge for many of these professionalized organizations was that they did not see themselves as immediately governable for external actors because they often had their own internal governance rules.

Academic organizations were seen as more fluid and fragmented through their ambiguous and often contested goals. Clients not only consume services but also have a voice in the decision-making process. Lines of authority are blurred and professional employees (i.e., professors) demand a high degree of autonomy in their work. Administrative processes are designed as support units for teaching and research (Riley & Baldridge 1977). Basically, these characteristics are still valid for describing colleges and universities of the 21st century (Sporn in Forest & Altbach 2007: 150). Recent changes in the environment of higher education show that it is necessary to adjust these models in order to explain organizational leadership structure, governance, and administration of today (Gumport & Snydman2002).

A quote from the 1970s depicts very nicely how universities were seen as not being able to become "normal" organizations:

> For some time people who manage organizations and people who study this managing have asked, "How does an organization go

about doing what it does and with what consequences for its people, processes, products, and persistence?" And for some time they've heard the same answers. In paraphrase the answers say essentially that an organization does what it does because of plans, intentional selection of means that get the organization to agree upon goals, and all of this is accomplished by such rationalized procedures as cost-benefit analyses, division of labor, specified areas of discretion, authority invested in the office, job descriptions, and a consistent evaluation and re-ward system. The only problem with that portrait is that it is rare in nature.

(Weick 1976: 1)

Universities may have been good examples of this description. Becher (1989) made interviews with academics and argues that academic values and knowledge structures within the disciplines are more important than formal structures. The same was true with the authority of the management of the universities: "Only the professors themselves were entitled to evaluate their own performance as a group of peers. The authority thus rested primarily with 'the visible and horizontal collegium' of chairholders" (Bleiklie 1999: 158).

Many of the university reforms changed all that. The formal structure changed establishing a formal hierarchy. Managers became hired from the outside, not elected among the peers within a university body. The formal structures also changed names. In Denmark, the old description "Konsistorium" changed to become "a university board"—just like any other board of an organization. Traditional modes of governance were changed dramatically and the internal democracy, once a proud feature of a traditional university, was being squeezed by these new developments. "In practice, elections of academic leaders have been abandoned in favour of appointed leadership, and representatives of students and staff have experienced reduced influence in institutional decision-making processes" (Maassen et al. 2009: 5). In general, academic employees at universities are seen as members of an organization and are expected to contribute to the goals of the organization (Bleiklie 1999: 517).

These changes made universities look more like other public and private organizations and making them less "incomplete".

Leadership and Management

"Making mangers manage and letting managers manage" (Kettl 1997) was always a key ingredient of NPM. By "breaking down bureaucracy", NPM was all about inserting managers into key positions in organizations, and giving them the tools to be risk-taking and performance-oriented managers, not bureaucrats with legal reservations and a focus on paperwork. The role of the public manager was largely based on the image of the CEO in a private sector company. Administrative positions grow and a large amount of resources are used on administration (Gornitzka, Kyvik & Larsen 1998; Ginsberg 2011). "Managerialism" in the public sector was described as a phenomenon already by Pollitt (1990). Today, the literature on higher education has found clear traces of what Seeber et al. (2015) calls a "managerial professional" model of governing universities.

An additional prominent element of modern colleges and universities is their leadership. With autonomy, deregulation, and decentralization, the power of rectors, presidents, and deans has increased (Sporn in Forest & Altbach 2007: 151). They gained more responsibility but also more accountability for their actions. Rectors or presidents can decide independently over budgetary and personnel issues. In general, the management team has more degrees of freedom to design and position the institution internationally. The board oversees their activities (ibid.). As institutions move towards more market-oriented, entrepreneurial models, governance will be concentrated more in the hands of the top leadership (ibid.). Studies of public sector leadership are prevalent in the public management literature at present (Bøgh Andersen et al. 2017).

To protect academic freedom and secure the legitimacy of Academia, the universities were highly self-governed under the Humboldt model. This made the formal management weak while the academics (the professors) were provided with autonomy. In this way the professors were the central, yet unformal, actors in the managerial system (Enders et al. 2013: 7). Recent reforms have in many ways redistributed the responsibility for management from the academics to a professional management (Enders et al. 2013: 8). The reforms have professionalized and empowered the formal university managements. The reforms have also formalized and intensified the steering dialog between ministries and universities, by setting up professional boards and performance goals (Christensen 2011).

The role of the (top) manager in NPM has been much researched in the literature. A current large research project led by Lotte Bøgh Andersen from the University of Aarhus explores the relationship between leadership and performance using an experimental design method. And Mark Moore's (1995, 2013) studies on how public managers seek to "create public value" was also centered around the individual leader or manager in the public sector. Later public governance studies, including the more network-oriented literature, has looked at the manager as a network manager (see Klijn & Koppenjan 2016), and how managers increasingly lead as part of a team or a wider network (Bryson et al. 2014; Bryson, Sancino, Benington & Sørensen 2017). One aspect of this is how public value is created in cross-sector collaborations. The lessons from the literature on strategic public management (Klausen 2014; Joyce, Bryson & Holzer 2014) are also highly relevant for the university sector.

Performance

The performance doctrine is today an integrated part of the universities. The performance management movement has developed strongly in the last three decades everywhere in the public sector. Performance measurement and management is perhaps the strongest trend that came out of the NPM reform agenda, and one which is likely to survive. As Donald Kettl observed many years ago, to set performance targets for what governments are doing, and then checking to see if those performance targets are met, is something that should not be so hard for governments to undertake, and a practice that taxpayers will find attractive because they then know what the government spends its money on.

Van Dooren, Bouckaert and Halligan (2010) are experts in performance studies, and they see performance measurement as "systematically collecting data by observing and registering performance-related issues for some performance purpose". They also add that "there could be a causal reason, e.g. there is a law or regulation which requires an organization to collect specific data. There could be an organizational objective, e.g. a need to use data for improvement" (ibid.: 6). Van Dooren, Bouckaert, and Halligan see performance management as "a type of management that incorporates and uses performance information for decision-making" (ibid.: 17).

The performance movement has been criticized from a number of perspectives. Radin (2006), writing from a critical political science perspective in her book on *Challenging the Performance Movement*, argued that decision-makers and public managers tend to forget about the role of politics when they plan elaborate performance measurement and management systems. Radin also warned that big performance systems are likely to be incomplete and therefore often involve risks.

Much has been written since on the role of performance measurement and management as a public sector management approach (for overviews, see Pollit & Bouckaert 2017; Talbot 2005). The debate and academic interest have shifted dramatically towards more systematic empirical studies of performance. Researchers such as Donald Moynihan, Larry Lynn, Laurence O'Toole, Gene Brewer, Lotte Bøgh Andersen, Mads Leth Jacobsen, Martin Bækgaard, Poul Aaes Nielsen, George Boyne, Richard Walker, and many others today conduct highly sophisticated and systematic studies on public sector performance that allow for much more precision and technical brilliance in the studies. Any performance measurement and management discussion must now involve a discussion on the recent empirical results. A new study by eminent performance management scholars focus on the relationship between performance regimes, external accountability, and internal learning (Van Loon & Jacobsen 2017).

Improved performance is a central goal of most reforms in the public sector (another goal is the more elusive "value for money"). Most reforms include managerial systems, for example performance management, which are designed to improve performance using clear goals, performance indicators, monitoring, incentives, rewards, and sanctions (Walker, Boyne & Brewer 2010: 26; Soss, Fording & Schram 2011). The rationale under performance measurement and management is that performance can be improved by shifting focus toward results rather than inputs or procedures. Furthermore, an appraisal of the outcomes will heighten the motivation among the employees and make them more efficient (Moynihan 2006, 2008). Thus a higher performance is expected to occur, when the managerial tools impact on the employees and they respond to the tools by changing their daily work routines. However, the employees' reactions to PM are still debated in the research (Noblet & Rodwell 2009; Opstrup & Pihl-Thingvad 2018). Performance is increasingly being tracked and measured in international rankings. It becomes a management responsibility for top management to secure a robust ranking position. In this area, universities again look like other organizations that are constantly being ranked for their performance. Ranking of overall public sector performance can be found in a variety of indexes now, including the World Bank's Governance Indicators, the OECD's "Governance at a Glance", the Bertelsmann foundations Sustainable Governance Index, the Corruption Perception Index (Transparency International), and most recently the International Civil Service Index from Oxford University.

The Following Chapters

This book contains ten chapters including the present introductory chapter.

Chapter 2:
Data and Methods
Niels Ejersbo, Pernille Bak Pedersen, and Signe Pihl-Thingvad

The chapter provides an overview of the different data sources used in the book and how these have been collected. It discusses the combination of quantitative and qualitative data used in the book and how this gives us a unique opportunity to cover the different aspects of university governance. It also includes a general discussion of methodological issues related to the data and analyses used in the book.

Chapter 3:
University Management and Reforms in Context—The Relationship Between University Reforms and General Reforms in the Public Sector
Carsten Greve and Niels Ejersbo

The chapter discusses how reforms at universities correspond with the more general reform tendencies in the public sector. Using the Danish case as a point of departure, the chapter provides an overview of central reform elements at universities, such as performance management, professionalized management, amalgamations, and incentive systems, and how these elements relates to reform labels such as New Public Management, Public Governance, and the Neo-Weberian State among others. The chapter asks how and why reforms at universities correspond with the more general reform tendencies in the public sector. The purpose is to understand how universities have been reformed during a 15-year period. The official reform proposals and legislation from the government will be documented and discussed. Using a theoretical approach on gradual institutional change in the tradition of Streeck and Thelen (2005), the chapter shows how reform elements are typically "layered" on top of each other in an incremental way that paves the way for a gradual change. The chapter ends by pointing to a new and more complex form of organization for the university where change is gradual, but persistent, and where several governance forms are wired into the current university structure today, which then again presents new and pressing challenges for university boards, university directors, and employees.

Chapter 4:
Controlling Autonomy: Governmental Regulation of Danish Universities From 1989 to 2015
Pernille Bak Pedersen

This chapter analyzes whether and how the government has used rules in the University Act and ministerial orders to govern universities before and after the introduction of the university reforms. We look at four different rule types in the University Act: production rules, performance rules, rules stating requirements, and rules delegating authority. The government uses these rule types to control universities' process or output, decrease the autonomy, or delegate authority, respectively. The rules in the University Act and ministerial orders from 1989 to 2015 are counted and content coded. The analysis of the written rules is supplemented with interviews with university managers and civil servants from the ministry. The chapter answers the following question: *How has the governmental regulation of Danish universities developed considering the introduction of reforms in 1992 and 2003?*

Overall, the Danish government continues to regulate the universities, but the way the state regulates the Danish universities has changed remarkably. The government has applied rules to implement university reforms, which includes an increase in the university autonomy and managerial authority. Especially after the Danish universities became self-governing in 2003, rules have paradoxically also been used to reestablish some control over the publicly funded universities—both on universities' output and processes.

Chapter 5:
Board Influence and Interaction With University Management
Niels Ejersbo and Carsten Greve

The literature on boards questions the influence and importance to boards (Van den Berghe & Levrau 2004; Farrell 2005). Are boards influential and do they have an impact on the governance of the university, or are they just "rubber stamps" with limited influence? We have asked actors on different levels at the universities about the influence of the board. In addition, we analyze this question by looking at how boards interact with the university management and how lower levels of the university management make reference to the boards' decisions and strategies.

Chapter 6:
Department Chairs—Modern Managers or Old Administrators?
Niels Ejersbo and Carsten Greve

Public sector management has been through tremendous changes over the past decades (Christensen & Lægreid 2007). The role has changed from a focus on administration and rule-following to a modern manager that develops strategies and uses performance information and modern technology to motivate employees. The question is how this development has influenced the department chairs. The chapter looks at how the role of department chair has changed, the recruitment of department chairs, their view on career opportunities, the management role of the department chair, the use of management instruments, and their view on management challenges.

Chapter 7:
Autonomy and Performance Contracts at Universities
Niels Ejersbo, Signe Pihl-Thingvad, and Maiken K. Westergaard

Universities have traditionally been described as "tribes", anarchies, or loosely couple organizations (Capano 2011). After periods with organizational reform they look more like other large public institutions with a bureaucratic hierarchy that runs from the top to the bottom of the university organization. A crucial part of the reforms is the implementation of a performance management system with performance contracts between the Ministry of Higher Education and Science and each university board. This "steering-at-a-distance" should give the university more autonomy and hold it accountable at the same time. However, public statements from different leaders at Danish universities and the evaluations of the University Act on the contrary suggest that this managerial structure has resulted in decreased autonomy and closer micromanagement (Ministry of Science 2009; Degn and Sørensen 2015). In this chapter we first take a closer look at the use of performance contracts at Danish universities and then search for possible explanations of why the use of performance contracts have resulted in less and not more autonomy. We suggest two type of explanations. First, the lack of autonomy can be a result of how the ministry uses the overall steering model. Second, it may also be accounted for by the way the performance contracts are designed and how university boards use the performance contracts in their steering process.

Chapter 8:
Academics and Performance Systems
Poul Erik Mouritzen and Niels Opstrup

The university sector has—like many other public organizations— implemented performance management systems with the purpose of measuring research output and quality. However, performance management systems can result in unintended consequences such as goal displacement, symbolic behavior, a lack of innovation, tunnel vision, and suboptimization (Van Thiel & Leeuw 2002; Moynihan, Pandey & Wright 2012). What if incentive systems are not implemented flawlessly? Could it be that management has an interest in keeping the rules unclear, ambiguous, and arbitrary? Or could it be that employees have different incentives and/or opportunities to seek or get information about the incentive system? What if you know about the system only if you by coincidence happened to be at a particular place at a particular time? This chapter use the bibliometric research indicator introduced at Danish universities as an example of a performance management system, and presents a thorough analysis of planned as well as unplanned effects of such a performance management system. The chapter exploits a set of unique data, surveying academics before and after the introduction of a performance management system (the bibliometric performance indicator) at Danish universities.

Chapter 9:
Modern Management and Working Conditions in Academia
Signe Pihl-Thingvad and Niels Opstrup

This chapter looks at how reforms and performance management instruments influence the work environment in academia. The introduction of performance management strategies are supposed to support the employees' motivation and satisfaction—which in turn are expected to make them improve their performance (quantitatively and/or qualitatively) (Fletcher & Williams 1996). However, increased focus on results and outputs can also create too big of a pressure to perform and may function as a stressor instead (Sewell, Barker & Nyberg 2012; Mather & Seifert 2011). Furthermore, PM as a management tool might clash with the existing organizational and cultural traditions at the universities shaped by being a highly specialized profession with strong professional norms, with professional autonomy based on academic freedom and peer review as the leading principles (Kristensen et al. 2011). This can create a misfit between the management instruments and the academics' work values, which instead are likely to increase the perception of stress among the academics (Opstrup & Pihl-Thingvad 2016). Thus, the reform and its management instruments may have an ambiguous impact on the academics' work environment. Therefore, this chapter focuses on the consequences of PM at the Danish universities in relation to the academics' perception of their psychosocial work environment and their stress levels (tested using a quantitative sample of 2,127 Danish university researchers. We will conclude by discussing the practical and theoretical implications of our findings.

Chapter 10:
Conclusion
Niels Ejersbo, Carsten Greve, and Signe Pihl-Thingvad

The concluding chapter takes stock of the main themes discussed in the previous chapters. How have reforms changed the governance of universities? What are the role and influence of boards at universities? Do department chairs act as modern managers? To what extent is there an established hierarchy where managerial instruments trickle down and have influence at all levels of the university? What are the consequences of reforms for academics and their work environment? The chapter sums up the lessons learned and discusses the consequences for the governance of universities and for the future research of university governance.

References

Becher, T. 1989, *Academic Tribes and Territories*, Open University Press, Buckingham.

Bleiklie, I. 1999, "The University, the State, and Civil Society", *Higher Education in Europe*, vol. 24, no. 4, p. 509.

Bleiklie, I., Enders, J. & Lepori, B. 2015, "Organizations as Penetrated Hierarchies: Environmental Pressures and Control in Professional Organizations", *Organization Studies*, vol. 36, no. 7, pp. 873–896.

Bleiklie, I., Enders, J. & Lepori, B. 2017, *Managing Universities: Policy and Organizational Change From a Western European Comparative Perspective*, Springer International Publishing, Cham, Switzerland.

Bleiklie, I. & Michelsen, S. 2019, "Scandinavian Higher Education Governance—Pursuing Similar Goals Through Different Organizational Arrangements", European Policy Analyses. Early view February 2019.

Bøgh Andersen, L., Bøllingtoft, A., Salomonsen, H.H., Würtz, A., Holten, A., Jacobsen, C. B., Westergård-Nielsen, N., Ladenburg, J., Bro, L.L., Nielsen, P.A., Eriksen, T.L.M. & Jensen, U.T. 2017, *Ledelse i offentlige og private organisationer*, Hans Reitzel, København.

Brunsson, N. 2013, "New Public Organisations: A Revivalist Movement", in *The Ashgate Research Companion to New Public Management*, eds. T. Christensen & P. Lægreid, Ashgate, Aldershot.

Brunsson, N. & Sahlin-Andersson, K. 2000, "Constructing Organizations: The Example of Public Sector Reform", *Organization Studies*, vol. 21, no. 4, pp. 721–746.

Bryson, J.M., Crosby, B.C. & Bloomberg, L. 2014, "Public Value Governance: Moving Beyond Traditional Public Administration and the New Public Management", *Public Administration Review*, vol. 74, no. 4, pp. 445–456.

Bryson, J., Sancino, A., Benington, J. & Sørensen, E. 2017; 2016, "Towards a Multi-actor Theory of Public Value Co-creation", *Public Management Review*, vol. 19, no. 5, pp. 640–654.

Capano, G. 2011, "Government Continues to Do Its Job: A Comparative Study of Governance Shifts in the Higher Education Sector", *Public Administration*, vol. 89, no. 4, pp. 1622–1642.

Christensen, T. 2011, "University Governance Reforms: Potential Problems of More Autonomy?", *Higher Education*, vol. 62, no. 4, pp. 503–517.

Christensen, T. & Lægreid, P. 2007, *Transcending New Public Management*, Ashgate, Surrey.

Christensen, T. & Lægreid, P. 2011, *The Ashgate Research Companion to the New Public Management*, Ashgate, Aldershot.

Cohen, M.D. & March, J.G. 1974, *Leadership and Ambiguity: The American College President*, McGraw-Hill, New York.

Degn, L. & Sørensen, M.P. 2012, "Universitetsloven fra 2003. På vej mod konkurrenceuniversitetet?", in *Dansk forskningspolitik efter årtusindeskiftet*, eds. K. Aagaard & N. Mejlgaard, Aarhus Universitetsforlag, Aarhus.

Degn, L. & Sørensen, M.P. 2015, "From Collegial Governance to Conduct of Conduct: Danish Universities Set Free in the Service of the State", *Higher Education*, vol. 69, no. 6, pp. 931; 946–946.

Dunleavy, P., Margetts, H., Bastow, S. & Tinkler, J. 2006, "New Public Management Is Dead—Long Live Digital-era Governance", *Journal of Public Administration Research and Theory*, vol. 16, no. 3, pp. 467–494.

Enders, J., de Boer, H. & Weyer, E. 2013, "Regulatory Autonomy and Performance: The Reform of Higher Education Re-visited", *Higher Education*, vol. 65, no. 1, pp. 5–23.

Farrell, C.M. 2005, "Governance in the UK Public Sector: The Involvement of the Governing Board", *Public Administration*, vol. 83, no. 1, pp. 89–110.

Ferlie, E., Musselin, C. & Andresani, G. 2009, "The Governance of Higher Education Systems: A Public Management Perspective", in *University Governance: West European Comparative Perspectives*, eds. C. Paradeise, E. Reale, I. Bleiklie & E. Ferlie, Springer, Dordrecht.

Fletcher, C. & Williams, R. 1996, "Performance Management, Job Satisfaction and Organizational Commitment", *British Journal of Management Banner*, vol. 7, no. 2.

Forest, J. & Altbach, P.G., eds. 2007, *International Handbook of Higher Education*, Springer, Dordrecht.

Ginsberg, B. 2011, *The Fall of the Faculty: The Rise of the All-Administrative University and Why It Matters*, Oxford University Press, Oxford.

Gornitzka, Å., Kyvik, S. & Larsen, I.M. 1998, "The Bureaucratisation of Universities", *Minerva*, vol. 36, no. 1, pp. 21–47.

Greve, C., Lægreid, P. & Rykkja, L.H. 2016, *Nordic Administrative Reforms: Lessons for Public Management*, Palgrave Macmillan, London.

Gumport, P.J. & Snydman, S.K. 2002, "The Formal Organization of Knowledge: An Analysis of Academic Structure", *The Journal of Higher Education*, vol. 73, no. 3, pp. 375–408.

Hammerschmid, G., Van den Walle, S., Andrews, R. & Bezes, P. 2016, *Public Administration Reforms in Europe: The View From the Top*, Edward Elgar, Cheltenham.

Hood, C. 1991, "A Public Management for All Seasons?", *Public Administration*, vol. 69, no. 1, pp. 3–19.

Joyce, P., Bryson, J.M. & Holzer, M. 2014, *Developments in Strategic and Public Management: Studies in the US and Europe*, Palgrave Macmillan UK, London.

Kettl, D. 1997, "The Global Revolution in Public Management: Driving Themes, Missing Links", *Journal of Public Policy Analysis and Management*, vol. 16, pp. 446–462.

Kerr, C. 1963, *The Uses of the University*, Reprint edn, Harper and Row, New York.

Klausen, K.K. 2014, *Strategisk ledelse i det offentlige: Fremskrive, forudse, forestille*, Gyldendal, København.

Klijn, E.H. & Koppenjan, J. 2016, *Governance Networks in the Public Sector*, Routledge, London.

Kristensen, J.E., Nørreklit, H. & Raffnsøe-Møller, M. 2011, *University Performance Management: The Silent Managerial Revolution at Danish Universities*, DJØF Publishing, Copenhagen.

Maassen, P., Larsen, I.M. & Stensaker, B. 2009, "Four Basic Dilemmas in University Governance Reform", *Higher Education Management and Policy*, vol. 21, no. 3, pp. 1–18.

Marginson, S. & Considine, M. 2000, *The Enterprise University: Power, Governance and Reinvention in Australia*, Cambridge University Press, Cambridge.

Mather, K. & Seifert, R. 2011, "Teacher, Lecturer or Labourer? Performance Management Issues in Education", *Management in Education*, vol. 25, no. 1, pp. 26–31.

Ministry of Science, Technology and Innovation. 2009, *The University Evaluation 2009*, Copenhagen.

Moore, M.H. 1995, *Creating Public Value*, Harvard University Press, Harvard.

Moore, M.H. 2013, *Recognizing Public Value*, Harvard University Press, Cambridge, MA.

Moynihan, D.P. 2006, "Managing for Results in State Government: Evaluating a Decade of Reform", *Public Administration Review*, vol. 66, no. 1, pp. 77–89.

Moynihan, D.P. 2008, *The Dynamics of Performance Management: Constructing Information and Reform*, Georgetown University Press, Washington, DC.

Moynihan, D.P., Pandey, S.K. & Wright, B.E. 2012, "Prosocial Values and Performance Management Theory: Linking Perceived Social Impact and Performance Information Use", *Governance*, vol. 25, no. 3, pp. 463–483.

Noblet, A.J. & Rodwell, J.J. 2009, "Integrating Job Stress and Social Exchange Theories to Predict Employee Strain in Reformed Public Sector Contexts", *Journal of Public Administration Research and Theory: J-PART*, vol. 19, no. 3, pp. 555–578.

Olsen, J.P. 2007, "The Institutional Dynamics of the European University", in *University Dynamics and European Integration*, eds. P. Maassen & J. P. Olsen, Springer, Dordrecht.

Opstrup, N. & Pihl-Thingvad, S. 2016, "Stressing Academia? Stress-as-offence-to-self at Danish Universities", *Journal of Higher Education Policy and Management*, vol. 38, no. 1, pp. 39–52.

Opstrup, N. & Pihl-Thingvad, S. 2018, "Does Setting Goals and Incentivizing Results Matter for the Psychosocial Work Environment?", *Public Performance and Management Review*, vol. 41, no. 4, pp. 815–834.

Osborne, S.T. 2010, *The New Public Governance?* Routledge, London.

Pollitt, C. 1990, *Managerialism and the Public Services: The Anglo-American Experience*, Basil Blackwell, Oxford.

Pollitt, C. & Bouckaert, G. 2017, *Public Management Reform: A Comparative Analysis—Into the Age of Austerity*, Fourth edn, Oxford University Press, Oxford.

Polyanyi, M. 1962, "The Republic of Science: Its Political, and Economic Theory", *Minerva*, vol. 1, no. 1.

Radin, B.A. 2006, *Challenging the Performance Movement: Accountability, Complexity, and Democratic Values*, Georgetown University Press, Washington, DC.

Radin, B.A. 2012, *Federal Management Reform in a World of Contradictions*, CQ Press, Washington, DC.

Riley, G.L. & Baldridge, J.V., eds. 1977, *Governing Academic Organizations: New Problems, New Perspective*, McCutchan Publishing Corporation, Berkeley.

Seeber, M., Lepori, B., Montauti, M., Enders, J., de Boer, H., Weyer, E., Bleiklie, I., Hope, K., Michelsen, S., Mathisen, G.N., Frølich, N., Scordato, L., Stensaker, B., Waagene, E., Dragsic, Z., Kretek, P., Krücken, G., Magalhães, A., Ribeiro, F.M., Sousa, S., Veiga, A., Santiago, R., Marini, G. & Reale, E. 2015, "European Universities as Complete Organizations? Understanding Identity, Hierarchy and Rationality in Public Organizations", *Public Management Review*, vol. 17, no. 10, pp. 1444–1474.

Sewell, G., Barker, J.R. & Nyberg, D. 2012, "Working Under Intensive Surveillance: When Does 'Measuring Everything That Moves' Become Intolerable?" *Human Relations*, vol. 65, no 2, pp. 189–215.

Soss, J., Fording, R. & Schram, S.F. 2011, "The Organization of Discipline: From Performance Management to Perversity and Punishment", *Journal of Public Administration Research and Theory: J-PART*, vol. 21, no. Supplement 2, pp. i203–i232.

Streeck, W. & Thelen, K. 2005, *Beyond Continuity: Institutional Change in Advanced Political Economies*, Oxford University Press, Oxford.

Talbot, C. 2005, "Performance Management", in *Oxford Handbook of Public Management*, eds. E. Ferlie, L. Lynn & C. Pollitt, Oxford University Press, Oxford.

Thiel, S.V. & Leeuw, F.L. 2002, "The Performance Paradox in the Public Sector", *Public Performance & Management Review*, vol. 25, no. 3, pp. 267–281.

Van Den Berghe, L.A.A. & Levrau, A. 2004, "Evaluating Boards of Directors: What Constitutes a Good Corporate Board?", *Corporate Governance an International Review*, vol. 12, no. 4, pp. 461–478.

Van Dooren, W., Bouckaert, G. & Halligan, J. 2010, *Performance Management in the Public Sector*, Routledge, London.

Van Loon, N.M. & Jacobsen, M.L. 2017, "Connecting Governance and the Front Lines: How Work Pressure and Autonomy Matter for Coping in Different Performance Regimes", *Public Administration*, vol. 96, no. 3, pp. 435–451.

Walker, R.M., Boyne, G.A. & Brewer, G.A. 2010, *Public Management and Performance: Research Directions*, Cambridge University Press, New York.

Weick, K.E. 1976, "Educational Organizations as Loosely Coupled Systems", *Administrative Science Quarterly*, vol. 21, no. 1, pp. 1–19.

West, D.M. 2016, *Megachange: Economic Disruption, Political Upheaval, and Social Strife in the 21st Century*, Brookings Institution Press, Washington, DC.

2 Data and Methods[1]

Niels Ejersbo, Pernille Bak Pedersen, and Signe Pihl-Thingvad

Introduction

The aim in this book is to describe and analyze university governance after the introduction of major reforms. The Danish universities serve as an illustrative case. In the last decades, the reform intensity around Danish universities has been high, with a significant reform in 2003. The purpose of the 2003 reform was to change the internal organization and management of the universities, and it has similarities to university reforms in many other European countries. A study with a single-country focus limits generalizability compared to studies including several counties (see Bleiklie, Enders & Lepori 2017). However, the similarity between the reform of Danish Universities and reforms in other countries, the unique set of data, and the combination of quantitative and qualitative methods makes the findings relevant for university governance in other settings. The focus on the Danish university case enables an in-depth understanding of the external and internal governance of universities after the introduction of major reforms.

Our perspective on university governance is inspired by organization theory and public administration. To understand the governance of the reformed Danish universities, we have investigated different levels of the organization—from the top management level to the employees, with a mixed methods approach. We use different types of data in order to cover the entire governance process. We have conducted surveys of board members, department heads, and researchers, and had interviews with heads of the boards, deans, department heads, researchers, and a few civil servants from the Ministry of Higher Education and Research. Furthermore, we have analyzed rules and development contracts. Reforms are not implemented from one day to the other and reform processes typically last for years. In order to analyze the governance process at universities, the surveys and interviews have taken place at least seven years after the reform of 2003.

In the following we describe the different data included in the book. The different chapters all draw on these data as their main source but may include additional data. The individual chapters construct specific measures and variables to be used in their analyses. Additional data and specific measures and variables are described in the respective chapters.

Data

The data were, except from the University Acts and ministerial orders, collected as part of a comprehensive research program—"Governing, Funding and Performance of Universities"—funded by The Velux Foundation. There has been a high degree of coordination when establishing the different data sets, and thus, the variety of data sets, and the mix of the qualitative and quantitative approaches, supplement each other. Table 2.1 is an overview of the data that form the basis of the analyses in this book.

Table 2.1 Data overview

Data	Collection	Population (N) and respondents (n)
QUESTIONNAIRE SURVEYS		
Survey with members of university boards	February–March 2014	$N = 81, n = 65$ Response rate = 80.2
Survey with department heads	September 2010– March 2011	$N = 181, n = 128$ Response rate = 70.7
	February–April 2015	$N = 160, n = 99$ Response rate = 61,9
Survey with researchers	January–April 2011	$N = 2,654$[1] Response rates for: Researchers excl. Ph.D.s = 59.0 Response rate Ph.D.s = 44.6
	April–May 2015	$N = 2,164$[2] Response rates for: Researchers excl. Ph.D.s = 35.1 Ph.D. students = 19.8
INTERVIEWS		
Interviews with chairmen of the university boards	Fall 2012–Fall 2013	Eight interviews One from each university Length of approx. one to two and a half hours.
Interviews with deans	September– December 2016	Seven interviews One from each university, one from the four overall academic fields.[3] Length of approx. one hour.
Interviews with department heads	September 2010– March 2011	64 interviews One from each of the 66 selected departments, two dropped out. Length of approx. 60–75 min.

(Continued)

Table 2.1 (Continued)

Data	Collection	Population (N) and respondents (n)
Interviews with researchers	November 2013– Spring 2014	44 interviews Four from 11 departments, selected among the 66 departments in the sample. Length of approx. one hour.
Interviews concerning development contracts	September–October 2015	Two interviews One interview with two civil servants from the Ministry of Higher Education and Research and one interview with two chief consultants from the secretariat at SDU.
DESK RESEARCH		
The University Act and ministerial orders	Valid University Acts and the entitled ministerial orders from 1989 to 2015 The number of words and subsections/ministerial orders is counted, and each subsection/ministerial order is content coded.	
Development contracts	Development contracts from 2005–2012 Each contract is content coded.	

[1] Sample of 66 departments.
[2] The sample for the 2015 survey is based on the 66 departments from the 2011 survey, but due to amalgamations, the sample only includes 59 departments.
[3] The four overall academic fields refers to the humanities, social science, natural and technical sciences, and health and medical science.

Sampling of Departments in the Study

In 2010, we identified 182 Danish university departments, divided between 32 faculties at eight universities in Denmark. At Roskilde University (RUC), Technical University of Denmark (DTU), and Copenhagen Business School (CBS) there is no organizational level in-between the vice-chancellor and the individual department. Therefore, these universities are considered as faculties when it comes to sampling. A minimum of two departments were drawn from each faculty, giving us a total sample of 66 departments. IT University of Copenhagen was dropped from the sample because it is organized as one single department, employing only 63 researchers. Later, two department heads (from two different faculties and different main area of research) abstained for participating in interviews.

Reforms and policy initiatives can be implemented in various ways at the different universities and faculties. To ensure the variation of universities and faculties, and hereby ensure diversity in the research traditions and surroundings (managers, internal policies, rules, and culture etc.) within the sample, the departments are selected by stratification.

Questionnaire Surveys

Between February and March 2014, all the 81 *board members* at the eight universities in Denmark were asked to fill out a web-based questionnaire. Sixty-five members responded, which give a response rate at 80 percent. The questionnaire includes the following topics: board member's background; motivation to be part of the board; the board's priorities, role, and decision-making process; and influences at the university. The board members were also asked to compare their experiences at the university board with experiences from other boards where they were members. Furthermore, the questionnaire includes questions regarding the university's strategy and strategy process, managers' and stakeholders' influence on board's decision-making, the work with the development contract, and the ministry's governance of the university.

We have surveyed the *department heads* twice through questionnaires with approximately four and a half years between. The first survey was carried out between September 2010 and March 2011, and the second survey between February and April 2015. All head of the departments were asked to participate. In September 2010, the department heads encompassed 181 people, and, in February 2015, there were 160 department heads at Danish universities. The response rate in the first survey was 70.7 percent (128 respondents) and the second had a response rate of 61.9 percent (99 respondents). The questionnaire contains questions about the department heads' backgrounds, priorities between different tasks, and views on researchers' motivation and political initiatives. Furthermore, the department heads were asked about the division of labour between the department and faculty, the dean's or faculty's use of management tools, and whether decisions, taken at other levels, influence the departments. The questionnaires we handed to the department heads together with a prepaid envelope after interviewing them.

We have investigated whether the respondents reflect the population at relevant variables. It is likely that the department heads' gender, university, and the main area of research can affect how the department head manages and perceives the governance of the university. Table 2.2 shows how they compare to the population on selected variables. In Table 2.3 we compare the number of respondents with the population at each university.

The questionnaire surveys of *researchers, including Ph.D. students,* were also collected twice—in 2011 and 2015. In mid-January 2011, all 4,984 researchers (including Ph.D. students) employed at the 66 sampled departments were asked to fill out a web-based questionnaire. We retrieved names, titles, and e-mail addresses from the departments' homepages. In addition to a number of background variables (e.g., gender, age, title, field of research), the questionnaire focused on publication strategies, the status attached to different types of publications, the weight of different

Table 2.2 Comparison between respondents and population, department heads, 2011 and 2015 survey

	Respondents	Population
Copenhagen University	28.1	25.6
Copenhaven Business School	7.0	7.8
Technical University Denmark	8.6	10.0
Roskilde University	3.9	3.3
University of Southern Denmark	18.8	16.1
Aarhus University	23.4	26.7
Aalborg University	8.6	10.6
Missing values	1.6	0.0
Sum	100	100
Humanity	16.4	14.4
Social Science	28.9	28.9
Natural Science and Technology	41.4	42.2
Health	11.7	14.4
Missing value	1.6	0.0
Sum	100	100
Female	21.9	18.3
Male	76.6	80.6
Missing value	1.6	1.1
Sum	100	100

Table 2.3 Comparison between respondents and population, department heads, 2015 survey

	Respondents	Population
Copenhagen University	26.3	27.0
Copenhagen Business School	9.1	9.4
Technical University Denmark	12.1	11.9
Roskilde University	5.1	3.6
University of Southern Denmark	21.2	17.6
Aarhus University	16.2	17.6
Aalborg University	10.1	12.6
Sum	100	100
Humanity	15.2	13.3
Social Science	23.2	28.3
Natural Science and Technology	40.4	40.3
Health	21.2	18.2
Sum	100	100
Female	24.2	25.8
Male	75.8	74.2
Sum	100	100

motivational factors, the perceptions of the departmental context and leadership, the incentives structure, the job situation, the career expectations, the weekly working hours etc. Studies have shown that web-based surveys yield lower response rates than traditional postal or mail questionnaires (Kaplowitz, Hadlock & Levine 2004). However, since computers are important working tools for university-employed researchers, it was considered to constitute less of a problem in the current case. Participation in web-based surveys is easier for frequent computer users (Bryman 2004). After administrating two reminders, the overall response rate was 53.3 percent. For staff in tenured or tenure-track positions it was 59.0 percent, whereas it only was 44.6 percent for Ph.D. students. However, Ph.D. students were only asked a subset of the questions in the questionnaire and do not enter into all of the analyses. The second questionnaire survey of the researchers was collected between April and May 2015. Researchers from the same 66 departments received a questionnaire. This time the number of researchers at the sampled departments were 7,397. Nonetheless, the number of respondents were a little lower in 2015 compared to 2011, as the response rate in 2015 was respectively 35.1 percent for staff in tenured or tenure-track positions and 19.8 percent for Ph.D. students. The lower response rates in 2015 is probably due to technical problems with the online survey program used for the survey.

We have compared the respondents with the non-respondents in the total sample (researchers at the 66 departments) for the two rounds of surveys. The comparison for the 2011 survey shows that the respondents and the non-respondents are very similar when it comes to gender, position, area of research, and universities. However, researchers from the Technical University of Denmark have a higher drop-out rate, and University of Southern Denmark has a lower drop-out rate compared to other universities. Ph.D. students have a lower response rate compared to other groups of employees. In general, there is a tendency to have a lower drop-out rate the more senior position the respondent has. The comparison for the 2015 survey between respondents and non-respondents shows that researchers from University of Southern Denmark, Social Sciences and the Humanities have answered the survey to a larger extent, whereas researchers from the Technical University of Denmark and from Health have a lower response rate.

For some variables, it is also possible to compare the respondents in the two surveys with the total population of researchers at Danish universities. In 2011, the two groups are comparable with the exception that Ph.D. students and researchers from the Technical University of Denmark are underrepresented while researchers from humanities are overrepresented. In 2015, there are noticeable differences between the respondents and the population. Researchers from the Technical University of Denmark are underrepresented while researchers from University of Southern Denmark, Social Sciences and Humanities, are overrepresented. To a lesser extent, researchers from Aarhus University are overrepresented while the Natural/Technical Sciences are underrepresented. All in all, the two surveys are somewhat representative of researchers at Danish universities, and despite the minor discrepancies we have not found it necessary to introduce weights for the analyses carried out in this book.

Interviews

The interviews were all semi-structured and guided by theoretically relevant topics and questions gathered in an interview guide. When the interviewer perceived it to be relevant, questions from the guide are followed up by additionally questions. After the collection process, the interviews were transcribed and content coded in the qualitative data analysis software NVivo.

We have interviewed all eight *chairmen of the university boards* at the Danish universities (this time including the IT University of Denmark). The interviews took place between Fall 2012 and Fall 2013. Prior to the interviews, the interviewer sought information about the specific university in statutes, minutes from board meetings, and self-evaluations. This enabled the interviewer to ask more qualified questions, and to receive a better understanding of the specific university. The chairmen of the boards were asked questions within the following topics: their motivation for entering the board, the composition and role of the board, the boards' work, their role in the strategy process, accountability, the boards' influence at the university etc. Each of the eight interviews lasted for between one and two and a half hours.

One *dean* from each of the seven sampled universities (i.e., all Danish universities excluding the IT University of Copenhagen) was interviewed. Besides the criteria of representation from the seven universities, the deans are selected so that the four main research fields are represented,[2] and all the interviewed have been deans for at least one year. The interviews gave valuable insight into the internal and external governance of the school/university. We covered the influence of the rector, the board, the external structures, and the policies on managerial decisions by the dean. We asked questions about the dean's role and tasks, the relationship with the rector, other deans at the university, and the department heads. We also touched upon the role of the board, and their influence on the strategy process and at the university in general. Furthermore, the interviews were about how the dean perceived the Ministry of Higher Education and Research's governance of the universities and the reform from 2003. At the end of the interview, we asked the dean to reflect upon whether and how the governance at the universities has changed after the reform from 2003. The seven interviews each lasted for approximately one hour.

During the Winter 2010–2011, intensive interviews were conducted with 64 of the 66 sampled *department heads* (two abstained from participating in the interviews). The interviews—lasting on average 75 minutes—focused on the management of the department, its organization, the use of financial incentives, performance indicators, and other management tools, the work environment etc.

Through interviews with 44 researchers, we have investigated researchers' publication behavior, the researchers' motivations, and how governance and incentive systems influence the researchers. In the selection of the researchers, we first selected 11 departments from the 66 departments, and subsequently we selected four researchers from the 11 departments. The interviews at each department covered at least one experienced researcher and one researcher who was relatively new within academia. Each of the 44 interviews lasted for approximately one hour.

After the collection and content coding of the development contracts, two interviews with four informants were collected in September and October 2015. One of the interviews was with two civil servants from the Ministry of Higher Education and Research, and the other interview was with two chief consultants from the secretariat at SDU. They all worked with the development contracts, and had done it for several years, but from different sides of the table. The interviews gave us insight into the process of the development contracts, their function, how they fit into the governance of the universities as a whole, and how the contracts have changed over time.

Desk Research

The Ministry of Higher Education and each university have entered into a so-called *development contract* on a regular basis since 2000. We have collected all the *development contracts* between the Ministry of Higher Education and Research and each university from 2005 to 2015. During that period each university entered in six contracts (2005, 2006–2008, 2008–2010, 2011, 2012–2014, 2015–2017), totaling 48 contracts. The contract contains a number of performance targets that the university must fulfill and must account for by the end of the contract period. In each contract, the number of targets are counted, and the targets are coded regarding measurability, content (two dimensions: external vs. internal and research, education, knowledge sharing, internationalization etc.), the type of goal (input, process, output, outcome), whether the goal is voluntary or mandatory to the university etc. The contracts are coded in Nvivo.

After the collection and content coding of the development contracts, we made two interviews with four informants in September and October 2015. One of the interviews was with two civil servants from the Ministry of Higher Education and Research, and the other interview was with two chief consultants from the secretariat at University of Southern Denmark. They all worked with the development contracts, and had done it for several years. The interviews gave insight into the function of the development contract, their role in the governance of the universities, and how the contracts have changed over time.

The governmental regulation of the universities is investigated by looking at different rules. We have made a content coding of the *Danish University Act and ministerial orders* from 1989 to 2015. As this investigation was not originally part of the research project, the methodological approach is fully described in Chapter 4.

In the investigation of the governmental rules and development contracts, both the objective (rules and contracts) and subjective (questionnaires and interviews) data make the foundation for the analysis. The information from different levels of the organization and the variety of data sources gives us an unique opportunity to get a broader view and understanding of the governance processes taking place at universities.

Notes

1. Part of this chapter is based on Mouritzen, Opstrup and Pedersen (2018) and Opstrup (2014).
2. The humanities, the social sciences, the natural and technical sciences, and health.

References

Bleiklie, I., Enders, J. & Lepori, B., 2017, *Managing Universities: Policy and Organizational Change From a Western European Comparative Perspective*, Springer International Publishing, Cham, Switzerland.

Bryman, A., 2004, *Social Research Methods*, Oxford University Press Inc., New York.

Kaplowitz, M.D., Hadlock, T.D. & Levine, R., 2004, "Comparison of Web and Mail Survey Response Rates", *Public Opinion Quarterly*, vol 68, no 1, pp. 94–101A.

Mouritzen, P.E., Opstrup, N. & Bak Pedersen, P. 2018, *En fremmed kommer til byen: ti år med den bibliometriske forskningsindikator*, Syddansk Universitetsforlag, Odense.

Opstrup, N. 2014, *Causes and Consequences of Performance Management at Danish Universities*, University of Southern Denmark, Odense.

3 University Reforms in Context— The Relationship Between University Reforms and General Reforms in the Public Sector

Carsten Greve and Niels Ejersbo

The chapter asks how and why reforms at universities correspond with the more general reform tendencies in the public sector. Using the Danish case as a point of departure, the chapter provides an overview of central reform elements at universities such as structural and organizational changes, performance management developments, professionalized management requirements, amalgamations, and incentive systems. The purpose is to understand how universities have been reformed during a 15-year period. The official reform proposals and legislation from the government will be documented and discussed. The chapter will track the particular changes from one reform proposal to the next, including the reform introducing boards and giving the rector/president more power, the structural reform merging universities that reduced the number from 12 to 8 universities in 2008, and the recent reform efforts aimed at securing competitive power in the international ranking game and the need to attract external funding from research councils and private sector companies and foundations. The chapter shows how universities have been reformed through a gradual and layered process making universities more geared towards both being ranked internationally and serving the purpose of the Danish industry and commerce. The second part of the chapter will ask how the specific university reforms are related to the wider and international reform trends associated with key governance forms such as New Public Management, New Public Governance, and the Neo-Weberian State. These reform trends have been documented both in international research (see for example Pollitt and Bouckaert's book on *Public Management Reform* [2017], and the recent COCOPS-project book on *Public Administration Reforms in Europe* edited by Hammerschmid, Van den Walle, Andrews and Bezes [2016]). Using a theoretical approach on gradual institutional change in the tradition of Streeck and Thelen, the chapter shows how reform elements are typically "layered" on top of each other in an incremental way that paves the way for a gradual change. The chapter ends by pointing to a new and more complex form of organization for the university where change is gradual, but persistent, and where several governance forms are wired into the current university structure today, which then again presents new and pressing challenges for university boards, university directors, and employees.

Theories of Public Management Reform

Understanding public management reform from a theoretical perspective is a prerequisite for analyzing how reforms unfolded in the Danish university context. Pollitt and Bouckaert (2017) present a useful starting point as their model, and their analysis of public management reform is often considered to be the classic reference in the academic reform literature. Pollitt and Bouckaert's (2017: 33) model consists of five elements: the socioeconomic context (global economic forces, sociodemographic change, socioeconomic policies), the political system (new management ideas, pressure from citizens, party political ideas), elite decision-making (what is desirable and feasible?), chance events, and the administrative system (content of the reform passage, implementation process, results achieved). Pollitt and Bouckaet put "elite decision-making" at the center of their reform model, and they stated that reforms in their perspective are mostly conceived of as a top-down process where key ministers and top civil servants play pivotal roles.

The reform model has stood its test of time (Pollitt and Bouckaert's book is now in its fourth edition since its original publication in 2000), but there are additions that can be made from recent research insights from the reform literature. First of all, Kamensky (2018) has reminded us that government reforms often have strong narratives that drive developments and that help convince skeptics about the consequences of reforms. A well-known narrative in the world of reform is "From red tape to results: creating a government that works better and cost less"; this was the title of the Clinton/Gore reform in the U.S. federal government in the 1990s. The reform was about getting rid of unnecessary bureaucracy ("cutting red tape") while promising a better public service at less cost for the taxpayers. Narratives have come to have a prominent place in the workings of reforms. Second, Mintrom and Luetjens (2017) have argued that the public value propositions set out at the beginning of a policy initiative or a reform period should be closely aligned to the actual public value produced later on. Reforms should consider how public value propositions can be implemented and how they can create public value (in the sense that Mark Moore [1995, 2013] advocated) later on. Too often, there has not be a link established between reform promises and reform results. Third, reforms are often political and it is no use to try to keep politics out of the equation, according to Radin (2012), if a realistic picture of a reform process must be painted. Fourth, there is often a reform entrepreneur (Mintrom & Luetjens 2017) that is the key actor in driving the reform forward. DeSeve (2012) has described how the reform entrepreneur can use a network approach to implementation. Fifth, reforms must have backing from key interests and must be prepared for pushbacks from opponents. If reformers are well prepared, they might introduce a whole new ball game, as Patashnik (2008) has described, to the implementation situation. Finally, Moore (2013) has described how public value creation must be the outcome of any change or reform process for public sector organizations.

The reform process takes place in a public sector with established institutions and actors in a highly institutionalized field. Change processes are therefore likely to be incremental and through institutional change mechanisms identified by scholars working with historical-institutional theory.

As can be seen (Figure 3.1), the original Pollitt and Bouckaert model on public management has added features, including the importance of narratives, the need for a better alignment of public value proposals and public value creation, the role of reform entrepreneurship, the key decision-making process with open policy windows, implementation through networks, and public value as an outcome of the reform process. This theoretical framework will be used in the following characterization of the reform development in the university sector.

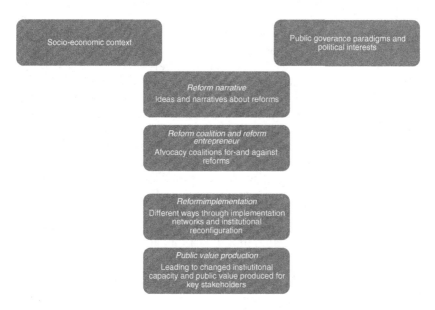

Figure 3.1 Theoretical reform model inspired by Pollitt and Bouckaert with added theoretical features

University Governance Reforms in Denmark

The reform episode this chapter is examining began in 2003 with a new University Reform. This was not the first reform of Danish universities. In 1970, a new University Act (Styrelsesloven) introduced institutional democracy in the wake of the 1968 student revolt (Hansen 2011) giving faculty, students, and other staff formal influence on the governance of the universities. The 1993 University Act maintained the overall governance structure, but gave rector and other leaders more power and introduced external members in the university senate. Performance contracts were introduced in 1999 (see Chapter 4) as an attempt to manage universities at arm's length (Kristensen et al. 2011). The changes and the reforms of the university sector are characterized as "dynamic inertia" (Hansen 2011) and some reform elements are more "muddling through" than part of a larger plan (Christensen 2017). It has been argued that the slow moving pace has changed and that the university sector during the past decade has been through radical reforms (Lind & Aagaard 2017). The 2003 reform marked on the one hand a new and different governance system at Danish universities but on the other it can be seen as a continuation of a development that started with the University Act in 1970 (Degn & Sørensen 2012).

A political agreement for a new structure for the universities was passed by Parliament in 2002 (Aftale om Universitetsreform—tid til forandring for Danmarks universiteter, oktober 2002). The University Reform in 2003 changed the legal status of the Danish universities from state institutions to self-governing institutions through a change in the Danish University Act. Universities had to establish new boards with a majority of external board members. The role of the "rector"/president gained more power than before where the role of the rector was very much dependent on the peer-dominated "Konsistorium" (Senate)—a collegial body that included academics as well as technical staff and student representatives. The 2003 change in the University Act must be seen in context with other structural reforms that began to be introduced at the time in Denmark. This is to say that the change for universities was not unique, but was part of a wider reform movement in the Danish public sector.

In 2006, the Danish government began to prepare for a new structural change in the university system. A report on "The University System in Denmark" (Danmarks Forskningspolitiske Råd 2006) pointed out that that global research context meant that structural change was needed. "Structure" referred to the number of universities, the size of a single university, the universities' geographical location, and the division of labor and collaboration possibilities between universities.

The mergers were decided in 2006 and began to be enacted January 1, 2007. The reform meant that 12 Danish universities were reduced to 8 universities. The eight remaining universities were these: University of Copenhagen, Aarhus University, Technical University of Denmark, University of Southern Denmark, Aalborg University, Roskilde University,

Copenhagen Business School, and the IT-University. The process began with the Minster of Research announcing in June 2006 to the universities in Denmark that they would have to consider mergers on a voluntary basis. The universities were given a deadline until September 2006 to come up with suggestions for mergers. The reform also included most of the governmental research institutes that were merged into the universities. The result was the new structure with eight universities that now included the governmental research institutes. The process are characterized as "voluntariness under compulsion" (Hansen 2011: 239).

An evaluation report of the reforms of the universities was published in 2009 called "Universitetsevaluering. Evalueringsrapport 2009" (Danish Ministry for Research). The mergers were expected to yield the following results: more cross-disciplinary collaboration on education, more flexible and relevant course catalogs for students, higher success rate for universities in applying for EU funding, higher quality understood as a better impact for universities, better collaboration between universities and private companies on innovation, and more effective knowledge production when merging applied research institutions into universities (Ministry of Research 2009: 41). For the research, the mergers were supposed to create stronger universities and to make universities more able to compete for funding in an age of globalization.

The report concluded on both university governance and on mergers. On university governance, the report concluded that universities had achieved more autonomy, but that there were also some points for observation, especially the risk of over-regulation/micromanagement. On the mergers, the report concluded both that the mergers had created many organizational change processes and that Danish research was doing well in the rankings (but that they were already doing well before the mergers). The report called attention to two questions that were still unanswered in relation to the mergers: (1) Did the mergers lead to more specific institutional research strategies profiles for each university and was the development going in the right direction? (2) What kind of diversity and profile did the mergers seek to encourage? The report asked if the development was heading towards one "Danish Universities" image with several sub-profiles, or more competition and uneven development with very different profiles and images was supported? See Figure 3.2 for the location of the universities after the mergers.

Regarding EU funding, the report concluded that Danish universities' high research quality led to many EU-funded projects, but that Danish universities did not yet seem to play an important role in the coordination FP7 projects, which were thought to be less ambitious. The report therefore recommended that Danish universities take a much more active role in seeking EU funding, and especially seek coordination responsibilities for large, EU-funded projects.

In 2009, the minister could announce that the goal of investing 1 percent of BNP in universities had been superseded, and that the government

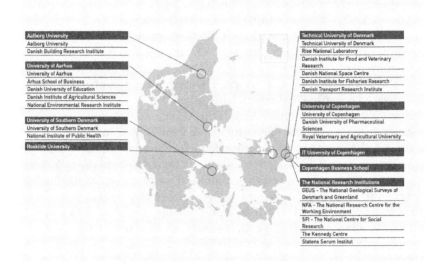

Figure 3.2 From the Ministry of Research Report (2009) (Universitetsevalueringen 2009)

wanted to invest six billion DKK more in universities to top the status of the record investment in universities ("Sander: forskningsmål er nået— med top på" Press release 25. august 2009).

The government was like other countries interested in assessing the quality of research and making universities compete for funding for research. Countries like Norway and Australia had already introduced a performance-based university research funding system (Mouritzen, Opstrup & Pedersen 2018), and in the Bibliometric Research Indicator was implemented in the Danish university sector (see Chapter 8 in this book). The Bibliometric Research Indicator is used to allocate funding to the universities based upon the number of registered publications. It was implemented gradually from 2011 and was considered controversial from the start. At the beginning, its reallocating effect was rather limited, but later on it has had a more substantial impact (ibid.).

In 2010, the Danish government announced a reform of the stipend program ("SU-støtte") for students receiving an education in Denmark. The Danish stipend program is generally regarded as one of the most ambitious in the world. The government wanted to make the stipend program more effective. ("SU-reform skal skabe vækst og beskæftigelse" Pressemeddelelse 19. November 2010"). The new stipend reform ("SU-reform") was made into law by parliament in 2013 ("SU-reformen er vedtaget"—Press release 28. Juni 2013).

In 2012, the Danish government introduces a new national innovation strategy with 27 new initiatives ("Regeringen præsenterer Danmarks nationale innovationsstrategi"—Press release 19. December 2012). In 2013, Parliament made a political agreement that led to the establishment of Innovation Fund Denmark (Danmarks Innovationsfond) that receives 1.5 billion DKK annually. This represented a thorough revision of the research and innovation system in Denmark ("Ny stor innovationsfond skal løse samfundsudfordringer og skabe arbejdspladser"—Press release 3. Oktober 2013).

In 2013, Parliament legislated on a reform ("Fremdriftsreformen") that made students finish their university studies quicker. An adjustment of the reform was agreed on 20 November 2015.

In 2016, the OECD's research barometer confirms that the impact of Denmark's research production is in the top three among the OECD countries. In 2016, Denmark was also at the top with regard to investment in research ("Dansk forskning har stor gennemslagskraft"—Press release 23. December 2016). The minister of research at the time, Søren Pind, commented that:

> In Denmark, we prioritize research highly because it is research that has to bring us into the future. That is why is it of utmost importance that Danish research is of a high quality and can be used by other researchers and the business sector. The verdict here shows that Danish research has great impact, and that research is relevant to businesses, and we should be proud of that.
>
> (Ministry of Research, Press release, 23. December 2016)

On April 11, 2017, Parliament agreed a policy for "Better management at the universities" ("Bedre rammer for ledelse af universiteterne"). The agreement had four components: (1) guidelines for the board's responsibilities, (2) guidelines for appointing external board members, (3) demands for competencies for external board members, and (4) strengthening dialog and use of performance contracts ("Politisk aftale om bedre rammer for ledelse på universiteterne "—Press release 11. April 2017).

In December 2017, it was announced that Denmark had got 5.2 billion DKK to 1,181 different research projects from the EU Horizon 2020 program since its start in 2014, and the ministry regarded this figure as satisfactory ("Dansk forskning runder 5 mia. støttekroner fra EU"—Press release 22. December 2017).

Explaining the Reform Pattern for Universities in Denmark

This section aims to analyze the reform patter that was described earlier from the reform theoretical model presented at the beginning of the chapter.

First, there was the socioeconomic context of globalization that led to the political idea of pursuing a globalization strategy for the university sector to make the universities in Denmark more robust, bigger in size, and able to perform and attract especially EU funding better for the future. This also included a substantial increase in funding—mostly as earmarked competitive funding. The government raised the investment in universities to 1 percent of BNP, which was seen as a remarkable raise. This meant that the government gave high priority to research and higher education policy. Second, in administration and governance terms, the Danish government's policy approach subscribed to a variety of governance paradigms. The reforms are characterized as the NPM-inspired reforms (Hansen 2011; Lind & Aagaard 2017) with an emphasis on competition, and universities were given more autonomy in order to make their own strategies on how to perform better. Students were offered a wider choice of courses and education opportunities with a more diverse profile. Students were mainly seen as customers who had to choose from different products that universities offered. At the same time there was an increased political interest in research and higher education with detailed regulation and reforms strengthening the influence of government. These characteristics are more in line with a Neo-Weberian State approach. The emphasis on collaboration with private companies and other actors outside academia and the need to create networks and alliances corresponds well with a New Public Governance paradigm. From a public administration paradigm perspective, it is clear that a number of different paradigms have influenced the reforms, and even though a New Public Management perspective is influential, it is more a mix of different approaches.

The reform narrative has been quite clear that Denmark needs to have bigger and better universities in order to compete for students and for EU funding. The need for more useful research and more interaction between universities and private companies were also part of the narrative driving reform initiatives. The Minister for Research and Innovation said in 2003 that universities should be more concerned about research that could be turned into solutions for private companies under the heading "from thought to invoice" ("fra tanke til faktura"). This narrative caused a lot of criticism (Hansen 2011), but it told in a simple way the idea behind the reforms. Today most universities have sections or independent organizations that link private business and faculty and students in order to create spinouts and make sure that new ideas and innovations are turned into business ideas.

The decision to go ahead with the reforms was largely an elite decision made by the Danish government and a majority in Parliament. The reform coalition consisted of the government and its coalition partners in Parliament. The consensus for reforming the universities came from most of the political parties in parliament (Hansen 2011). There is also some evidence to suggest that the bigger universities were in favor of a strengthened role for universities. The smaller universities might have been skeptical at first at the sight of mergers which would threaten their existence.

The implementation of the merger reforms progressed as the universities were actually merged, but it was a long process that was, for the most part, also characterized by conflict (Lind & Aagaard 2017). The Ministry of Research was driving the reform implementation forward, and the formal merger happened quite fast so that within less than a year—from the summer of 2006 to the winter of 2007—the mergers were a reality. However, long processes within the different institutions followed the merger, and for some it resulted in major changes of the internal organizational structure (Hansen 2012).

The question is this then: Were the goals achieved and public value produced? The 2009 evaluation report by an external evaluation committee suggested that the goals of the reforms had been met to a large degree, but that there were also some questions that still needed answered. In terms of the public value of giving more autonomy to universities, which allows them to act more freely in pursuing whatever strategic moves they see fit, the report concluded that more autonomy had been granted to universities, but also that there was a risk of over-regulation/micromanagement on behalf of the university vis-à-vis the universities. The lack of autonomy given to the universities has been pointed out several times, and the ministry has been criticized for continuing the same regulatory regime (Hansen 2010; Christensen 2017—see also Chapters 4 and 7 in this book).

After the reforms, the universities have been criticized for spending too much on administration and management. In 2010 the Ministry of Higher Education and Science asked PricewaterhouseCoopers to establish comparable data of the cost of managing the universities. There was a considerable variation in the costs used to manage and administrate the universities (Ministry of Higher Education and Science 2011). Christensen (2012, 2017) has analyzed the administration and management at the Danish universities and shows both how the administration and management levels at the Danish universities have grown much faster than the increase in faculty and that there is a similar trend when it comes to salaries for management positions.

With regard to the goal of making universities bigger by merging them and making them more robust in order to improve their research and their intake of funding, the 2009 report concluded that research environments had improved, which was witnessed by the improved position in international rankings, and that universities attracted more funding from the EU, but the report also noted that Danish research already had a good standing before the mergers, and that the increased amount of funding did not lead to Danish universities taking on coordinating roles in large EU projects.

Also the institutional capacity of Danish universities seems to have been improved, but it is difficult to say if this was a cause of the reforms. Later initiatives have been put in place to adjust the reforms, for example by establishing a bigger Innovation Fund and by adjusting the guidelines for selecting external board members to the universities' boards, and the student reforms ("Fremdriftsreformen") that should make students go through their university education much faster.

The reforms seem to have developed in a bell-shaped curve, where the initial reforms of performance contracts and changes to the legal status of self-governance entities with new boards (with external board members) and the wish to increase the autonomy then culminated with the peak position of the merger reform in 2007. This is when universities got bigger in order to attract more students and to be in a better position to compete for EU funding and be in better positions in international rankings. Thereafter, there were the adjustments on board governance and membership, the guidelines for leaders and managers, and the logical continuation of bigger-is-better policies (Innovation Fund and Fremdriftsreformen). This move combined the Neo-Weberian State governance idea of a stronger state with the competitive features of the New Public Management. The reform movement in the university sector got off to an ambitious start, then peaked with the mergers, and is now in a process of consolidation, which also means that the policy priority may have been dampened by the government. It is now more about consolidation than new initiatives. See Figure 3.3 for an overview of the university reforms.

How can we understand reform development in an institutional change perspective? The reform could be seen as layering process where different layers were added to the reform as time went on. The initial movement was the performance contracts in the late 1990s that connected the university closer to the Ministry of Research. The bigger decision was the political move to change the legal status of the university by changing the University Act and making the universities self-governing entities with a board dominated by external members and giving more power

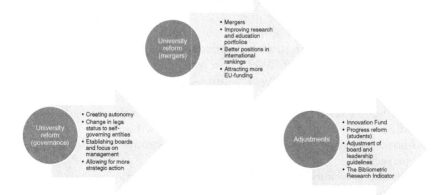

Figure 3.3 University reforms in Denmark

to the rector/president who became more like a CEO. This allowed for more strategic action to be taken by the rector and the board in unison, which fitted the government's political strategy at the time. This could be interpreted as a focus on competition and simulating what private sector companies are doing in line with the New Public Management paradigm in governance. The next layer in the change process was the mergers in 2007 when universities got bigger in size and had more personnel, which enabled them to compete more for EU funding in close competition with universities elsewhere in Europe. The recent reform elements do not represent new layers as such, but are more logical consequences of the government's policy laid out earlier. The progress reform aims to make students even more competitive and to get them through their studies faster, thereby saving money. The adjustment of board and leadership guidelines announced in 2017 can be seen as corrections to the institution of the board, not a completely new way of governing universities. The recent years have also witnessed a less ambitious investment policy in universities, although the government of the day will continue to emphasize that universities have high political priority. The universities' strategies are closer aligned to the Danish state's governance strategy and therefore resemble the Neo-Weberian State mode of governance associated with a stronger state. The future will surely bring new reforms, but they will be what we have called "adjustments". The overall organizational structure of the university organization is set, and future reforms will take place within the frame of the current organizational structure.

Conclusions

This chapter has traced the reform development in Danish universities since the early 2000s. The question then is this: Were the reform elements just layered on top of each other without any meaningful order, or were the different elements fitted together to form a unified approach to university governance? To a large degree, the approach taken by the government did fit into a coherent policy narrative that was characterized by the following features: (1) The governance structure of the universities should be reorganized to conform towards more "complete" organizations (in the sense described by Brunsson & Sahlin-Andersson 2000; Bleiklie, Enders & Lepori 2017 and others) with a self-governing legal status, a board with external members and a strategy-oriented rector/president that acts more like a CEO than a traditional university administrator. (2) The university sector should consist of fewer but larger universities with enough capacity to compete for research funds (especially EU funds for Denmark's universities) and to offer a wide variety of educational subjects to the students who should act more like users/customers. (3) The public value produced should be better research as measured in international rankings and a plate of educational opportunities. The universities are also seen as a driver for economic development in society through innovation and continued education. They must interact more with the private sector and society and show that they are useful. The government has played the part of the key reform entrepreneur with a parliament. The potential opposition to the plans in universities and elsewhere has not been able to mobilize a coalition against the government and the ministry. Research and higher education are now policy areas that have political attention, and political parties use research and higher education to position themselves. The larger universities may have benefitted from the reforms as the larger universities grew in size and capability during the reform period. Together, this reformed university is to be a competent knowledge producer with strong entities in the individual university, but it should also form a coherent university sector in Denmark that can carry out the ambitions set out by the narrative of a more competitive and robust university by the government and parliament. The reforms at Danish universities fit descriptions of reforms carried out in other countries (see, e.g., Bleiklie et al. 2017; Stensaker, Välimaa & Sarrico 2012), but they are also more radical from a comparative, international perspective (Hansen 2011), which makes it interesting to follow the results and further reform developments in the Danish university sector.

References

Bleiklie, I., Enders, J. & Lepori, B. 2017, *Managing Universities: Policy and Organizational Change From a Western European Comparative Perspective*, Springer International Publishing, Cham, Switzerland.

Brunsson, N. & Sahlin-Andersson, K. 2000, "Constructing Organizations: The Example of Public Sector Reform", *Organization Studies*, vol. 21, no. 4, pp. 721–746.

Christensen, J.G. 2012, "Magt og management på universiteterne", in *Hvordan styres videnssamfundet? Demokrati, ledelse og organisering*, eds. J. Faye & D.B. Pedersen, Nyt fra samfundsvidenskaberne, København.

Christensen, J.G. 2017, "Frihedens bureaukratisering", in *Styring og evaluering i den offentlige sektor*, eds. E.M. Ghin, C.H. Grøn & M.B. Kristiansen, Hans Reitzels Forlag, København.

Danmarks Forskningspolitiske Råd. 2006, *The University System in Denmark*, Danmarks Forskningspolitiske Råd.

Degn, L. & Sørensen, M.P. 2012, "Universitetsloven fra 2003. På vej mod konkurrenceuniversitetet?", in *Dansk forskningspolitik efter årtusindeskiftet*, eds. K. Aagaard & N. Mejlgaard, Aarhus Universitetsforlag, Aarhus.

DeSeve, E. 2012, *Managing Recovery: A View From Inside*, IBM Center for the Business of Government, Washington, DC.

Hammerschmid, G., Van den Walle, S., Andrews, R. & Bezes, P. 2016, *Public Administration Reforms in Europe: The View From the Top*, Edward Elgar, Cheltenham.

Hansen, H.F. 2010, "University Reforms in Denmark and the Challenges for Political Science", *European Political Science*, vol. 10, no. 2, pp. 235–247.

Hansen, H.F. 2012, "Fusionsprocesserne: Frivillighed under tvang", in *Dansk forskningspolitik ved årtusindskiftet*, eds. K. Aagaard & N. Mejlgaard, Aarhus Universitetsforlag, Aarhus.

Kamensky, J.M. 2018, "Looking Back Over My 45 Years of Involvement With Government Reform Efforts", *Public Administration Review*, vol. 78, no. 2, pp. 305–310.

Kristensen, J.E., Nørreklit, H. & Raffnsøe-Møller, M. 2011, *University Performance Management: The Silent Managerial Revolution at Danish Universities*, DJØF Publishing, Copenhagen.

Lind, J.K. & Aagaard, K. 2017, "Danske universiteter efter reformbølgen: fra makro-reformer til intra-organisatorisk forandring", in *Styring og evaluering i den offentlige sektor*, eds. E.M. Ghin, C.H. Grøn & M.B. Kristiansen, Hans Reitzels Forlag, København.

Ministry of Higher Education and Science. 2011, *Analyse af de administrative omkostninger til generel ledelse og administration i 2008 og 2009 på de danske universiteter*, Ministry of Higher Education and Science, Copenhagen.

Ministry of Science, Technology and Innovation. 2009, *The University Evaluation 2009*, Copenhagen.

Mintrom, M. & Luetjens, J. 2017, "Creating Public Value: Tightening Connections Between Policy Design and Public Management", *Policy Studies Journal*, vol. 45, no. 1, pp. 170–190.

Moore, M.H. 1995, *Creating Public Value*, Harvard University Press, Harvard.

Moore, M.H. 2013, *Recognizing Public Value*, Harvard University Press, Cambridge, MA.

Mouritzen, P.E., Opstrup, N. & Bak Pedersen, P. 2018, *En fremmed kommer til byen: ti år med den bibliometriske forskningsindikator*, Syddansk Universitetsforlag, Odense.

Patashnik, E.M. 2014; 2008, *Reforms at Risk: What Happens After Major Policy Changes Are Enacted*, Princeton University Press, Princeton.

Pollitt, C. & Bouckaert, G. 2000, *Public Management Reform: A Comparative Analysis*, First edn, Oxford University Press, Oxford.

Pollitt, C. & Bouckaert, G. 2017, *Public Management Reform: A Comparative Analysis—Into the Age of Austerity*, Fourth edn, Oxford University Press, Oxford.

Radin, B. 2012, *Federal Management Reform in a World of Contradictions*, CQ Press, Washington, DC.

Stensaker, B., Välimaa, J. & Sarrico, C.S. 2012, *Managing Reform in Universities: The Dynamics of Culture, Identity and Organisational Change*, Palgrave Macmillan, Basingstoke.

Streeck, W. & Thelen, K. 2005, *Beyond Continuity: Institutional Change in Advanced Political Economies*, Oxford University Press, Oxford.

4 Controlling Autonomy

Governmental Regulation of Danish Universities From 1989 to 2015

Pernille Bak Pedersen

Introduction

In the last several decades, the Danish government has introduced several university reforms. The primary aims of the reforms have been to improve the governance of universities by deregulation, increase university autonomy and managerial authority over organizations' processes, and increase output control. However, it is uncertain how the governmental regulation has actually developed and whether the government has fulfilled the intended deregulation and decrease in process control.

The government has formulated the intentions behind the Danish university reforms in two important bills (Bill No. 75, 1992/1; Bill No. 125, 2002/1), resulting in new university acts in 1992 and 2003 (Act No. 1089, 1992; Act No. 403, 2003). Many aspects of the university reforms intend to change the governance of universities and are inspired by the normative ideas of performance management (Moynihan 2008: 26–38). The overall aims of the reforms can be seen from the ministers' presentations of the bills. A central aim is to increase the university performance by de-bureaucratizing the governance of universities, decentralizing the authority and accountability to university managers, and increasing the university autonomy. Specifically, the government intends to set the universities free from the state hierarchy, simplify the rules that regulate the universities, professionalize the university management, establish development contracts between the minister and universities, and establish performance information systems.

From the literature, we know that governance reforms, such as performance management reforms, also have to be implemented and put into action. Scholars have observed that the national context and former governance forms influence the outcome of the governance reforms (Pollitt & Bouckaert 2011; de Boer et al. 2017). Modern governance reforms intending to debureaucratize and deregulate the public sector have shown to result in a reregulation (Hood 1999). Similarly, another line of research observes an increasing rather than a decreasing number of rules (Schulz 1998; Van Witteloostuijn & de Jong 2009; Jakobsen &

Mortensen 2014). Furthermore, intentions of increasing the managerial authority on how to increase performance in decentralized public organizations have shown to be unsuccessful in several cases. Studies indicate that political executives tend to reestablish control over the processes, while public organizations and managers do not receive the promised autonomy and authority over processes (Maor 1999; Moynihan 2008: 39–57).

In this chapter, I will answer the following question: *How has the governmental regulation of Danish universities developed considering the introduction of reforms in 1992 and 2003?* The governmental regulation is studied as a policy instrument (Vedung 2010). I analyze whether and how the government has used rules in the University Act and ministerial orders to govern universities before and after the introduction of the university reforms. I have observed four different rule types in the University Act: production rules, performance rules, rules stating requirements, and rules delegating authority. The government uses these rule types to control universities' process or output, decrease the autonomy, or delegate authority, respectively. I have counted and content coded the number of rules in the University Act and ministerial orders from 1989 to 2015. The analysis of the written rules is supplemented with interviews with university managers and civil servants from the ministry.

Overall, the Danish government continues to regulate the universities, but the way the state regulates the Danish universities has changed remarkably. The government has applied rules to implement university reforms, which includes an increase in the university autonomy and managerial authority. Especially after the Danish universities became self-governing in 2003, rules have paradoxically also been used to reestablish some control over the publicly funded universities—both on universities' output and processes.

Theoretical Framework: University Autonomy and Governmental Control

Regulation is here understood as a policy instrument. One way to investigate the government's regulation of universities is to analyze whether the policy instrument is applied. A *policy instrument* is here defined as a set of techniques by which governmental authorities wield their power (the definition is inspired by Bemelmans-Videc, Rist & Vedung 2010: 3). The instruments can be used by different governmental authorities, such as the parliament or a ministry, and can target different groups, such as citizens or administrative actors in the public sector (Bemelmans-Videc et al. 2010: 3–4). In this study, I am interested in how the Danish Parliament and the Minister of Higher Education and Research regulate the Danish universities and university managers.

Regulation, subsidies, and information are policy instruments in Vedung's typology of instruments, also noted as sticks, carrots, and sermons (Vedung 2010). Regulation is defined as "measures undertaken by governmental units to influence people by means of formulated rules and directives which mandate receivers to act in accordance with what is ordered in these rules and directives" (Vedung 2010: 31). This conceptualization differs somewhat from the broader English understanding of regulation, which also refers to orders, norms, standards, etc. (ibid.).

Regulation varies in content. Vedung distinguishes between a negative formulation prescribing certain phenomena or actions vs. a positive formulation proscribing what has to be done (Vedung 2010: 41–42). Furthermore, prohibitions can be ordered according to their strength and whether they include conditions (ibid.). One example is enabling legislation, which is a prohibition aiming at controlling or raising demands on the activity involved (ibid.). Jakobsen and Mortensen have analyzed the rule development in the act regulating the Danish primary schools and have identified the following two types of rules: production rules and performance rules (Jakobsen & Mortensen 2016). *Production rules* regulate the process of what an organization should deliver in its service production and how, while *performance rules* regulate performance, either directly by specifying targets or indirectly by establishing metrics or information systems. These two rule types differ regarding their control over process vs. output.

Regulation is the traditional instrument of the government and is exposed to criticism for being rigid, burdensome, and ineffective—both in the public debate and the scholarly literature. Consequently, governments have sought to deregulate and replace rules with other policy instruments. As described in the following sections, the deregulation movement does not, in overall terms, result in a shift away from governmental regulation, a decrease in the governmental control over public organizations, or a decrease in the number of rules.

Performance Management

As Moynihan puts it: "we are in an era of governance by performance management" (2008: 3–25). Public managers are asked to justify their actions in terms of the outcomes they produce, they are expected to do more with less, and the public sector must constantly seek new ways to foster performance. Performance management is both a normative and descriptive theory, whereas the normative intentions of the doctrine have shown to differ substantially from how the performance management–inspired reforms are implemented in practice (Moynihan 2008).

The normative doctrine of performance management offers solutions to the perceived weaknesses of the traditional rule-bound governance (Moynihan 2008: 26–38). The traditional and hierarchical public organization is criticized for being inefficient, ineffective, and inflexible. It is claimed that public managers in traditional public organizations are restricted by central regulation on input and processes, and managers are hereby too focused on aligning with rules and maximizing inputs instead of complying with goals and improve performance (Moynihan 2008: 28–31).

A central mantra in the doctrine is the potential of enhancing the performance in the public organization by changing from a rule-based governance of input and process to directing the attention towards organizational achievements (Boyne 2010) and decentralizing decision-making to managers with a close knowledge of the problems and processes (Moynihan 2008: 34). The central agency should define goals in measurable terms and create performance information systems (Boyne 2010: 207–226; Moynihan 2008: 26–38). Managers should use the performance information to make more informed and rational decisions. Autonomy and authority should be delegated to decentralized managers of public organizations who have the knowledge of how to enhance performance in the specific organization, and managers should be held accountable for the centrally set targets.

In the descriptive literature about how performance management reforms are implemented, a study finds that the Danish government applies rules to implement performance management initiatives. Concurrently, the government controls the decentralized public organizations' service production with rules (Jakobsen & Mortensen 2016). Several scholars have observed a *partial adoption* of performance management in different contexts (e.g., Moynihan 2008: 39–57). The government has created performance management systems and mandated agencies to create and disseminate performance requirements. However, a focus on performance and managerial accountability is not always followed by an increase in the managerial flexibility and authority (Moynihan 2008: 39–57). Moynihan suggests political executives to be guided by the costs and benefits of the reforms and the symbolic benefits of performance management reforms to be the primary reason for the introduction of such (Moynihan 2005, 2008: 58–74). Maor explains how an increase in managerial authority over the implementation of policies implicates a loss in control for political executives. Paradoxically, this loss can make political executives hunger for more control over bureaucracy, which can lead to less managerial authority (Maor 1999).

Reforms

The normative ideals and intentions of reforms are often different from how reforms are implemented in practice (e.g., Pollitt & Bouckaert 2011). A paradigmatic shift away from the rule-bound bureaucracy to a new ideal form of governance is questioned (e.g., Olsen 2006). Rather than a shift away from one paradigmatic governance form to another, scholars point to a *layering* effect of different forms of governance and different types of policy instruments (Lægreid, Roness & Rubecksen 2006; Christensen, Lie & Laegreid 2008; Christensen & Lægreid 2011). Regulation is the traditional instrument associated with the bureaucratic governance form. Governments attempt to replace the bureaucracy and regulation with new forms of governance and policy instruments. Nonetheless, the expected result is a mixed governance form; that is, the government still uses regulation together with other policy instruments.

In Pollitt and Bouckaert's analysis of how public management reforms are implemented in different countries, they find that the national context influences the implementation. Pollitt and Bouckaert argue that the Nordic countries are moving towards a Neo-Weberian State (Pollitt & Bouckaert 2011: 118–122). The argument is that "Neo elements" such as an increasing orientation towards meeting citizens' needs, encouragement of achieving good results, and a professionalization of the managers are implemented, while "Weberian elements" coexist. The Weberian elements refer to a reaffirmation of the role of the state as the main facilitator, the role of the representative democracy, and the role of the administrative law. Similarly, de Boer et al. (2017) find university reforms to be influenced by the national context they are translated into. Furthermore, studies across policy domains point out that deregulation is followed by a reregulation (Hood, James, Jones, Scott & Travers 1999; Vedung 2010: 10–11), and the regulation inside the government (e.g., the state's regulation of public organizations) is observed to increase rather than decrease (Hood et al. 1999). ·

Although the national context and historical trajectories are expected to influence the implementation of reforms, the development of the state's governance of universities across countries are observed to develop in similar directions (Capano 2011). In four countries, Capano has observed a development towards a steering-at-a-distance. By examining the Danish University Act, and with inspiration from Olsen's typology (Olsen 2007), Degn and Sørensen (2015) find changes in the visions and governance of Danish universities over time. They suggest universities both to be controlled and free as the state shapes and guides the universities through a "conduct of conduct", for instance, through development contracts and an accreditation institution (Degn & Sørensen 2015). Hence, it is relevant to analyze the development of different rules in the University Act and how the government delegates authority, states requirements, and controls universities' performance and processes.

Rules

From the rule literature, we will expect the number of rules to increase until there is a rule saturation (Schulz 1998; Van Witteloostuijn & de Jong 2009). It is easier to establish new rules rather than remove existing ones. Two different rule dynamics are suggested as the underlying processes by which rules are created and changed and, hereby, as the explanation of the increasing number of rules.

First, scholars suggest rules to be solutions to *problems*, whereas organizational learning is the dynamic of rules (Zhou 1993; Schulz 1998; March, Schulz & Zhou 2000). When the organization perceives a new problem, which could be problems with the educational quality at the universities, the organization solves the problem, either by changing existing rules or establishing new rules. Accordingly, an increase in the number of rules is an indication of experienced problems that the organization seeks to solve.

Second, scholars suggest *interests* to be the dynamic of rules (Jennings, Schulz, Patient, Gravel & Yuan 2005; Van Witteloostuijn & de Jong 2007, 2008, 2009). Stakeholders promote and protect their interests by establishing new rules or maintaining or changing existing rules. If the Parliament and minister are interested in influencing universities, they are expected to do so by rules. For instance, the government and minister can be interested in improving the quality of the university educations. Not only are political executives expected to improve their interests through the establishment of rules, but also universities, university management, and the universities' interest group are expected to enhance their interests through rules. For instance, Danish universities may be interested in receiving authority to supply educations internationally, and employees from the universities or interest groups can lobby politicians to establish such rules. Other interest groups, such as representatives for businesses and industries, also have interests in the university sector. Therefore, they can also be expected to lobby for specific rules improving their interests.

A so-called competency trap (Levitt & March 1988: 322–323) may explain why we expect governments to solve problems and improve interests by rules despite the intention of diminishing the number of rules. Political executives are accustomed to govern and influence the society by the establishment of rules in laws and ministerial orders. In the Danish ministries, legal offices still exist, primarily consisting of civil servants with a legal background trained to formulate rules. This can lead to a competency trap caused by path dependencies of the ministries' arrangements, and politicians and civil servants' traditions and norms of how to govern. From this argumentation, the Parliament and minister are expected to govern universities with the traditional policy instrument (i.e., regulation) in the traditional manner (i.e., on universities' processes).

The Methodological Approach

The government's formal and written regulation of the Danish universities primarily appear in the University Act and ministerial orders. Therefore,

I have mainly focused on the development in the regulation based on these documents. As the formal and written rules may differ from how the rules are practiced, the investigation of the Act and orders are supplemented with interviews with civil servants from the ministry and managers from the university.

I have demarcated the examination by investigating acts, consolidating acts (laws that combine existing laws), and ministerial orders. The Parliament can issue new acts, while the minister can have a mandate in the act to issue ministerial orders. Both acts and ministerial orders are binding for the public administration and citizens in Denmark. As ministerial orders are important politics but politicians are not as involved in the production of these rules as in the production of laws, ministerial orders have been characterized as "policy without politicians" (Page 2012 in Jakobsen & Mortensen 2014: 37).

Furthermore, I have delimited the examination to investigate the University Act (formerly titled the Government Act) and related ministerial orders because I am interested in the government's direct regulation by rules of the universities and university managers. Several legal documents regulate universities indirectly. This may be the regulation of agencies with relevance for the universities, such as regulation of research councils and foundations (e.g., Act No. 346 24/05/1989), the accreditation institution (Act No. 294 27/03/2007), and the Danish Evaluation Institute (Act No. 2090 12/05/1999). These actors are important for the universities, and the legal framework may be so as well, but the legal documents regulating these actors do not encompass a direct regulation of the Danish universities and university managers by the Parliament/minister. These documents are therefore not included in the quantitative examination of the rule development.

To analyze the governmental regulation in the period from before to after the introduction of university reforms in 1992 and 2003, I have counted and content coded the rules in the University Act and ministerial orders from 1989 to 2015. I have collected the University Acts and ministerial orders from the website "Retsinformation.dk". "Retsinformation" is an online collection of all Danish laws and ministerial orders. For each of the 27 years, the University Act and ministerial orders applicable at the end of the year are collected. The analyzed acts are shown in Table 4.1.

For each year, I counted the number of words and subsections in the University Acts as well as the number of, and words within, the ministerial orders. For instance, §1.1, §1.2, and §1.3 are counted as three subsections. By counting both words and subsections/ministerial orders, I measure the number of regulations with two measurements in the University Act and ministerial orders, respectively. As illustrated in Figures 4.1 and 4.2, the two measurements follow a similar pattern with a high correlation between the two measurements. When the number of

Table 4.1 Governmental and University Acts
valid between 1989 and 2015

Act, number, and date

Consolidation Act, No. 358 of 26/05/89
Act No. 1089 of 23/12/92
Act No. 154 of 31/03/1993
Consolidation Act No. 334 of 27/05/93
Consolidation Act No. 1048 of 23/12/98
Act No. 348 of 02/06/1999
Consolidation Act No. 1177 of 22/12/99
Act No. 403 of 28/05/03
Act No. 337 of 18/05/05
Consolidation Act No. 280 of 21/03/06
Act No. 544 of 08/06/06
Act No. 295 of 27/03/07
Consolidation Act No. 1368 of 07/12/07
Act No. 538 of 12/06/09
Consolidation Act No. 985 of 21/10/09
Act No. 728 of 25/06/10
Consolidation Act No. 754 of 17/06/10
Act No. 634 of 14/06/11
Consolidation Act No. 695 of 22/06/11
Act No. 1372 of 28/12/11
Consolidation Act No. 652 of 24/06/12
Act No. 1236 of 18/12/12
Consolidation Act No. 367 of 25/03/13
Act No. 623 of 12/06/13
Act No. 898 of 04/07/13
Act No. 520 of 26/05/14
Act No. 750 of 25/06/14
Consolidation Act No. 960 of 14/08/14
Act No. 1377 of 16/12/14
Consolidation Act No. 261 of 18/03/15

Source: Retsinformation.dk

subsections/ministerial orders increase or decrease, the number of words also increase or decrease with approximately the same number.

Each subsection is content coded from two rule systems, each rule system encompassing two rules types. Accordingly, I have observed and content coded four rule types in the University Act. The first rule system concerns governmental process control (production rules) and output control (performance rules), and the second rule system concerns regulation of managerial authority (rules delegating authority) and governmental control (rules stating requirements). Examples of the four rule types appear from Table 4.2.

Jakobsen and Mortensen (2016) have identified the first rule system, consisting of production and performance rules, and the definitions of

Table 4.2 Four rule types

Rule types	
Production rules	Control over universities' production Examples:
	§4.1 *The university may offer the following research-based fulltime programmes, which are independent, complete study programmes:1) Bachelor programmes for 180 ECTS points. 2) Master's (candidatus) programmes for 120 ECTS points. 3) PhD programmes for 180 ECTS points.* (2003) §9.1 *The university offers students guidance during their studies on the programme and their employment opportunities.* (2003) §13.1.2 *The university must promote a dialogue between the employer panel and the university on the quality and relevance to society of the programmes and must involve the employer panel in the development of new and existing programmes and in the development of new forms of instruction and examination.* (2007)
Performance rules	Control over universities' output by goal setting, establishment of Performance Systems, or metrics Examples:
	§10.8 *The board enters into a development contract with the Minister.* (1999) §10.3 *The Board shall administer the university's funds to ensure that they serve the university's goals to the greatest extent possible.* (2003) §19.2 *Subsidies for the approved programmes offered by the university in Denmark pursuant to section 4, subsection (1), nos. 1) and 2), and section 5 are provided on the basis of the rates laid down in the annual Appropriation Acts and the number of active fulltime equivalents and, if relevant, the number of completed* studies. (2007)
Rules stating requirements	Control over universities and/or university managers (i.e., the university board or rector) Examples:
	§2.4 *The university shall contribute to ensuring that the most recent knowledge within relevant disciplines is made available to non-research-oriented higher education.* (2003) §12.2 *Together, the members of the Board shall use their experience and knowledge concerning education, research and the dissemination and exchange of knowledge to contribute to the promotion of the university's strategic work.* (2003) §26.2 *The university must claim full payment for participation in teaching and in tests and other forms of assessment forming part of the exam in respect of part time and fulltime programmes to the extent that no grant or scholarship for the activity has been provided, cf. section 19, subsections (1), (8) and (10), and section 20, subsection (1).* (2011)

Rule types	
Rules delegating authority	Increase in the managerial or institutional authority Examples: *§21.2 The university may accumulate subsidies to be spent in accordance with the university's proper purpose in the following financial year.* (2003) *§4.1 The university may offer the following research-based fulltime degree programmes as independent and complete degree programmes: i) Bachelor's degree programmes comprising 180 ECTS credits. ii) Master's degree programmes comprising 120 ECTS credits. iii) PhD degree programmes comprising 180 ECTS credits.* (2003) *§18.8 In the charter, the Board may decide to set up Study Boards at different levels of the organization.* (2003)

the two rule types appear from the theoretical section. This rule system is also observed in the analysis of the University Act.

Each subsection in the Act from 1989 to 2015 has been systematically analyzed and coded as a performance rule, production rule, or neither. The prevalence of these two rule types indicates whether the government increases its focus on universities' performance and output control through the Act, according to the intentions of performance management, or whether the government regulates how universities deliver their service production and, hereby, perform process control, according to a more traditional and bureaucratic governance form. Theoretically, production rules can both contain requirements on how universities organize and provide their educations *and* how they organize and do research. However, in the University Act and ministerial orders, only a few subsections regulate the universities' research, and the production rules mainly regulate the universities' education, including how they ensure high quality and relevance of the educations.

In the examination of the University Act, I have identified another rule system consisting of the following two rule types: rules stating requirements and rules delegating authority. *Rules delegating authority* are almost similar with what Vedung describes as enabling legislation (2010: 42), although rules delegating authority is not necessarily a prohibition, which Vedung suggests enabling legislation to be. For instance, this rule type can give universities the mandate to supply education and issue certificates, and rectors the mandate to hire and fire managers for the scientific units at the university. Such rules can be formulated as follows: "The university/rector/boards *may* . . ." followed by what they have a mandate to do. The observation of rules delegating authority is an important nuance and contribution to the understanding of the government's regulation of universities because it illustrates that rules do not always restrict organizations' and managers' autonomy. However, the delegating rules vary in the degree of autonomy that universities and university managers receive. Sometimes, whether and how the universities use the received authority is voluntary, and other times, a delegation of authority is followed by several requirements to whether and how the authority is used. In such cases, the subsection is both coded as a rule delegating authority and a rule stating requirements.

Rules stating requirements are subsections containing one or more requirements to the Danish universities, the university boards, and/or rectors. This rule type is in some cases formulated as follows: "The university/rector/board *shall/must* . . ." followed by the requirement that they must fulfill. For instance, this rule type may contain a requirement to the universities to cooperate with the surrounding society and to contribute to the development of the international cooperation. The presence of this type of rule is an indication of the government enacting control over universities and university managers. Although such rules formally control the university and university managers, the degrees to which the rules affect the university and university managers' behavior differ. For example, the universities might have cooperated with the surrounding and international society even without the existence of the rules. Other rules are more restrictive and affect the universities to a greater extent. Rules stating that the superior should hire and fire university managers instead of employees electing them is an example of a sample of rules that have had a substantial influence on the universities.

For each subsection, I have assessed whether the subsection regulates the organizations' production and performance, states requirements, and/or delegates authority. The subsection is thus coded as none, one, or several of the four rule types. The four types of rules are *not* mutually exclusive or exhaustive. As a result, some subsections are not characterized as any of the four rule types. For instance, a subsection controls how the state funds the universities. This subsection regulates the state, not the universities and their managers, and is therefore not coded as any of the four rule types. Oppositely, some subsections are coded as more than one type of rule. Often, a subsection is coded as two rule types, one from both rule systems: a production/performance rule and a rule stating requirements/delegating authority. As already mentioned, a subsection can also encompass both a delegation and a requirement. In a few cases, one subsection delegates authority, states a requirement, and regulates the production/performance. Consequently, such subsections are coded as three rule types. In the University Act, no subsections regulate both the universities' production and performance. Accordingly, a subsection is characterized as three rule types as a maximum.

Besides the examination of the written rules, I have interviewed five civil servants from the Ministry of Higher Education and Research: one working with universities' legal foundation (e.g., the University Act and ministerial orders), two working with the governance of universities, and two managers within the ministry. From the university management, I have interviewed one rector, one former head of the board, and one university director. These interviews were collected between December 2015 and January 2016. As part of the research project "Governance, Funding and Performance of Universities" funded by the Velux Foundation, colleagues and I collected interviews of seven deans between September and December 2016. Through the interviews, I have investigated and analyzed how the government uses and how the university management receives the formal, written rules and the changes appearing from the University Act and the ministerial orders. The interviews help us understand how the governmental regulation of universities is practiced and why the government still uses rules and controls universities' processes after the introduction of the performance management-inspired university reforms.

Analysis: Governmental Control Over the More Autonomous University

Reregulation: Regulating From a Distance

The government's regulation of universities has changed remarkably during the period from 1989 to 2015. Through the University Act, the government has changed the scope of the state's governance of universities. The government has distanced itself to the universities, and the Parliament has formally professionalized and strengthened the university management against the employees and ministry and—from a distance—reestablished control over the universities.

In 1992, the University Act (Universitetsloven, Act No. 1089, 1992) replaced the so-called Government Act (Styrelsesloven, Act No. 271, 1970) from 1970/1973 (with the latest change in 1989). This replacement not only concerns the title; most rules in the Government Act were replaced with new and different rules. The new rules have strengthened the university management, both vis-a-vis the university employees (i.e., collegial agencies) and the government—a development also experienced by the interviewed. The rector, who is part of a managerial hierarchy to deans, heads of studies, and department heads, became responsible for both internal and external affairs. The management received authority from the government over the internal organization, the supply of educations, the intake of students, and the prioritization of the economy.

In 1999, the government introduced the development contracts by establishment of a rule in the University Act (§2.3 in Act No. 1177, 1999), and in 2003, the contracts became mandatory. The contracts can be understood as a new means or policy instrument that the state uses to govern universities. Compared with rules and economic incentives, civil servants in the ministry do not perceive contracts as an effective and efficient means to govern the Danish universities. The common view among the interviewed civil servants is that universities oblige to rules, and the ministry sanctions violations of law. If politicians wish to make sure that universities realize a political goal, regulation is selected as the most efficient policy instrument. The civil servants and university managers believe that contracts improve the dialog between the government and the universities, match their expectations, and are a tool for negotiation between the government (represented by the minister) and university managers at the specific institutions. Furthermore, civil servants from the ministry describe how the government uses contracts, regulation, and subsidies as supplementing instruments in their governance of universities. For instance, the government has used contracts, economic incentives, and rules to reduce the study duration. As the political executives do not find the contracts and economic incentives to be sufficiently effective and efficient, the government also regulates to ensure goal achievement.

In 2003, the government passed a new University Act (Act No. 403, 2003). This time, many of the existing rules from 1992 survived, and the Act from 2003 covers the same topics as the Act from 1992. However, some rules were adjusted and relatively many new rules were added. Again, the government strengthened the university management vis-a-vis the ministry and employees. University boards, with a majority of external representatives, replaced the collegial governing body and became the supreme authority at the university and responsible to the minister. Furthermore, university management was professionalized. Before, collegial organs elected the managers, and, after the reform in 2003, superior managers received authority to hire and fire the subordinated manager(s). The strengthening of the university management is not only a formal change but is also experienced in practice by the interviewed employees, both in the ministry and in the university managements.

One of the altered rules in the 2003 law is of great importance for the state's governance of the universities. With an alteration of §1.2, the Parliament changed universities' legal status from state institutions to self-governing institutions. The self-governance implies that universities are no longer part of the ministerial hierarchy. In order for the minister to issue rules concerning the self-governing universities, the minister needs a delegation of authority from the Parliament. Internal orders from the ministry, such as circulars, are not binding on the universities after 2003 (Kulturministeriet et al. 2009). The ministry, minister, and government have hereby created distance from the universities.

According to an interviewed legal employee from the ministry, the change from state-owned to self-governing universities has a major influence on the ministry's possibilities to govern and the state's actual governance of Danish universities. For instance, the legal employee explains how the government dimensioned university educations when the universities were state-owned institutions, and, after the self-governance, the government needed a mandate in the University Act to do so. Some of the rules established in the University Act after 2003 are topics that the government has formerly governed through the ministerial hierarchy.

Even though the state has created distance from the universities, the Parliament still has the authority to regulate the self-governing universities through the University Act. After 2003, the Parliament has increasingly used this authority, primarily by changing and establishing rules. As the Parliament has established more rules in the University Act than it has removed, the number of subsections and words have increased in the aftermath of the university reform from 2003 (see Figure 4.1). The increasing number of rules in the University Act can be characterized as a reregulation of the governance inside government (i.e., of the universities).

The steep upward curve in Figure 4.1 is broken by a decrease in the number of rules in 2011. The theory on rules indicates that it is difficult to remove rules. It is therefore interesting to look deeper into why it has been possible here. In 2006, the Parliament initiated the Danish University Evaluation, which was carried out by an international panel between December 2008 and November 2009. The panel took the intentions behind the reforms from 2003 and the university merging in 2007 as a frame of reference and, among other things, evaluated the university merging, the codetermination for employees and students, and the degrees of freedom (autonomy) (Ministry of Science Technology and Innovation 2009). Regarding universities' autonomy, the panel found that the achieved autonomy and improved decision-making capacity of universities were accompanied by a "dense set of rules and regulations, many of them too detailed" (ibid.: 10). The panel recommended a

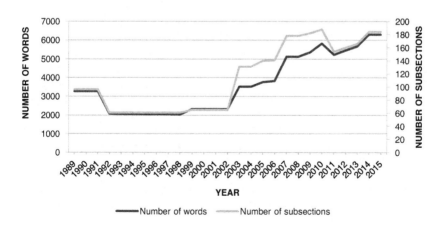

Figure 4.1 The development in the number of words and subsections in the University Act from 1989 to 2015

"high-trust strategy" and that politicians and implementing authorities should stick to overall strategic targets and leave the decision on how to reach targets to the universities.

With reference to the panel's recommendations, a deregulation of Chapter 3 of the University Act about governance of the universities is suggested in a bill from 2010, which was passed in 2011. The Parliament hereby removed rules regarding the internal organization, and the rector and board received authority on how to organize the universities. The panel's recommendations seem to enable the elimination of rules and a decrease in the total number of rules in the University Act from 2010 to 2011. Nonetheless, the number of rules was already back to the 2010 level in 2014.

Besides using the University Act to regulate the universities directly, the Parliament can also delegate authority to the minister, who can hereby regulate universities through ministerial orders. In contrast to the development in the University Act, the number of ministerial orders and words in the ministerial orders have decreased in total. The number decreases in the period between 1989 and 1996, and in 2003 (see Figure 4.2). The ministerial orders have changed from regulating educations at specific departments in separate ministerial orders to a less detailed and more general regulation of all educations at all universities. As the number of ministerial orders decreased, the tendency from specific to general regulation implicated an increase in the average number of words in the ministerial orders. In other words, the number of ministerial orders has decreased, but the ministerial orders consist of more words on average after 2003.

The period from 1996 to 2001 (see Figure 4.2) differs from the rest of the period with a notable increase in the number of ministerial orders. The establishment of specific ministerial orders regulating continuing

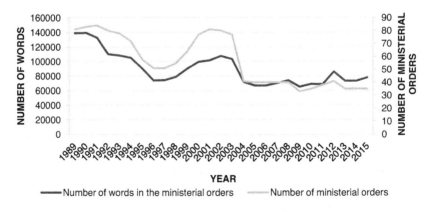

Figure 4.2 The development in the number of words in the ministerial orders and number of ministerial orders from 1989 to 2015

education (i.e., Master's and Diploma degrees) mainly causes the increase in the number of ministerial orders. The change from specific to general ministerial orders also concerns the ministerial orders regulating continuing education, and, from 2009, only two orders regulate continuing education.

Whether this development indicates a general trend in all Danish acts and ministerial orders can be questioned. To answer this question, I have compared the relative development in the University Acts and ministerial orders with the development in all Danish acts and ministerial orders. Jakobsen and Mortensen (2014) have kindly delivered the data on the general rule development in the Danish acts and ministerial orders. The increase in the number of words in the University Act with 60 percentage points from 1989 to 2011 is not exceptional for the Danish acts. The rule development in the Danish acts have increased steadily, with a total increase of 82 percentage points but with a high variety between different policy areas.

Jakobsen and Mortensen point to several conditions that influence the rule development in the Danish acts: national politics (left- or right-winged government), the EU, and modern reforms such as performance management reforms, self-governance, and liberalization. In all Danish ministerial orders, the number of words has increased with 147 percentage points between 1989 and 2011. This contradicts with the ministerial orders to the University Act, whereas the number of words has *de*creased with 51 percentage points in the same period. The comparison indicates that the Parliament has been relatively more engaged in regulating the university sector compared with other areas. The reregulation of the Danish universities therefore primarily seems to be politically rather than administratively driven.

So far, I have only touched a little upon the remarkable increase in subsections and words in the University Act after 2003 (Figure 4.1). From governing through the ministerial hierarchy, the universities have become self-governing institutions. However, the government still regulates the universities but now from the distance. In order to assess the content of the increasing number of rules after 2003, I will analyze the development in the four different rule types: rules delegating authority, rules stating requirements, performance rules, and production rules.

Governmental Control Over the Self-Governing Universities

In the aftermath of the university reform from 2003, the Parliament used the Act to strengthen the university managers' authority on the one hand and, on the other, to reestablish governmental control. The increasing authority and governmental control can be seen from the development in the different types of rules in the University Act.

Delegating Authority and Stating Requirements

Figure 4.3 illustrates a strong correlation between the number of rules delegating authority and the number of rules stating requirements. The government's delegation of authority to universities and university managers strongly correlates with its requirements to universities and university management. More authority to the university managers calls for more governmental control.

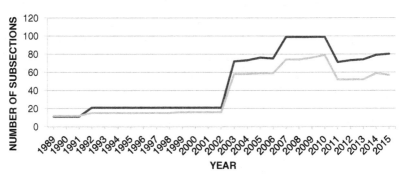

Number of subsections containing requirement(s) to universities, university boards or rectors
Number of subsections containing delegation of authority to universities, university boards or rectors

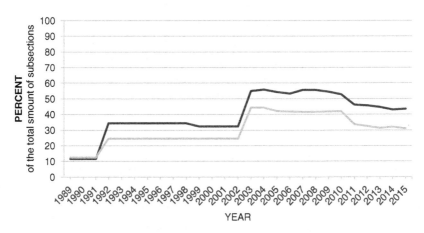

Percentage of the total number of subsections containing requirement(s) to universities, university boards or rectors
Percentage of the total number of subsections containing delegation of authority to universities, university boards or rectors

Figure 4.3 The development in the number of rules containing requirements or delegation of authority to universities and university managers in the University Acts from 1989 to 2015

Typically, a delegation of authority is followed by requirements, either in the same subsection, in the same section, or in the same chapter of the Act. The correlation between delegations and requirements is partly caused by an increase in subsections comprehending both a delegation and a requirement to universities and university management. For instance, in one subsection, the government delegates authority to universities for them to prioritize their economy, and, in the same subsection, the government requires universities to comply with grant provisions and rules of disposition. By stating requirements in the Act, the government reestablishes some control from the distance, and universities' autonomy and managerial flexibility to use the received power is hereby restricted.

The share of subsections that include a delegation of authority have increased from just above 10 percent to above 30 percent. The share of subsections that include requirements have increased from just above 10 percent to above 40 percent (Figure 4.3). From the University Act, it appears that the universities and their managers have received authority over the organization of the universities and the prioritization of the economy. After 2003, the government has to a larger extent also delegated authority to internationalize as internationalization became a salient topic (e.g., Statsministeriet 2006; Uddannelses- og Forskningsministeriet 2009). For instance, the government has delegated authority to increase universities' possibilities for exchange students and supply educations internationally in cooperation with foreign universities. As universities' authority increases, the government increases the control over the publicly funded universities. For instance, the governmental control concerns the requirement that universities must spend publicly funded resources in accordance with the intended purpose and make sure that the state receives the universities' net capital if the university board decides to close down the university.

An improvement of the quality and relevance of the higher educations has been a politically salient issue after 2003 (Uddannelses- og Forskningsministeriet 2013). This is reflected in the University Act. The universities have received authority over the educations they supply and the students they enroll. Historically, the universities have had a high degree of authority and autonomy over the content and methods of research and teaching. The Expert Committee on the Quality in Higher Education in Denmark has assessed the possibilities of improvements regarding study duration, completion, and employment rates, as well as the intensity of the educations. The funding system has been criticized for not supporting quality and relevance in education, and the universities have been criticized for focusing too much on increasing the amount of money they receive for the number of enrolled students (from the taximeter system). Regulation to improve the quality and relevance of education counts for several of the new production rules after 2003.

Performance and Production Rules: Governmental Control Over Universities' Output and Process

The Parliament's increasing focus on the self-governing universities' performance and the increasing governmental control over output do not necessarily lead to a decrease in the rule-based process of control. This is evident from the regulation of universities' production in the University Act. Oppositely, the number of both performance and production rules has mainly increased in the Act from 2003 to 2015, with a higher increase in the number of subsections regulating universities' education than the increase in subsections regulating universities' performance.

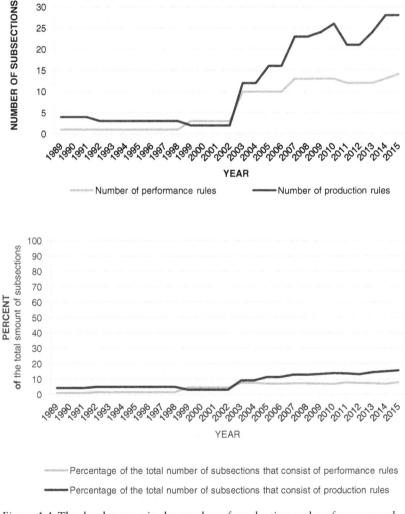

Figure 4.4 The development in the number of production and performance rules in the University Acts from 1989 to 2015

The share of subsections regulating universities' performance is in the whole period less than 10 percent, while the share of subsections regulating universities' production in the examined period comprises less than 20 percent of the Act (Figure 4.4). Despite a small share of these rule types, the development over time is substantial, with less than five subsections regulating production before 2003 and more than 25 subsections regulating the production in 2015. The production rules can theoretically encompass process control of both research and education. However, the regulation of universities' research through the University Act is limited to only a few rules, whereas Parliament's regulation of university education in the University Act has increased considerably.

The increase in the number of performance rules primarily reflects the following changes: the introduction of development contracts in 1999; the specification of targets for the university, university boards, deans, and department heads in 2003 and 2006; the establishment of a performance information system in 2014; and the government ensuring that the ministry can obtain performance information from the universities on the quality and relevance of their educations. All of these changes are formally an increase in the governmental output control.

The increasing number of production rules from 2003 primarily reflects an increase in the regulation of how universities should improve the quality and relevance of their educations and internationalization of university educations. The government has not been confident with universities' efforts to ensure high quality and relevance of their educations. Therefore, the government has established rules regulating how they should do so. For instance, the government requires that universities should offer students supervision about the education and the employment possibilities and supervision to students who are delayed. The government's arguments for these amendments were to increase the completion and employment rates. Another governmental initiative to increase the educational relevance was to require that universities should appoint recruitment panels represented by external members.

Danish universities showed an interest in supplying education internationally, and, by law, the government ensured that the universities obtained the possibility to internationalize and, at the same time, they made limitations and requirements to control the universities' spending on international students and foreign activities. For instance, Parliament established a main rule limiting universities to offer educations in Denmark, but with several exceptions: universities obtained the possibility to supply parts of their education internationally in cooperation with a foreign university and to exchange students with foreign universities.

Dynamics of the Rule Development

In the interviews, university managers describe how the governmental control is undesirably high and how they experience the governmental regulation to be too rigid and detailed. It is plausible that the actual development in the government's regulation did not live up to university managers' expectations, which were shaped by the wording in the bills and argumentation of the university reforms, emphasizing universities' freedom and autonomy from the state. However, some of the university managers also express an understanding for the need of a certain amount of governmental control of the universities, for instance, with reference to university managers' lack of goal achievements and the increasing amount of public funding to the university sector.

With reference to the Act, civil servants from the ministry describe the ministry's role as a supervisory authority. This includes, for instance, the establishment of a legal setting regulating universities to spend the publicly funded resources appropriately with a politically desirable outcome, ensuring an equal and fair treatment of students and sanctioning a violation of law. Students' rights are used as an example in interviews: a legal employee underlines the importance of the ministry ensuring students' rights, both by shaping the legal framework and sanctioning a violation of law. A university manager exactly exemplifies that such rules are sometimes too rigid and inflexible.

Moreover, civil servants in the ministry serve the minister and government, who represent the Danish people. They seek to influence the universities in the politically requested direction—a direction that is not always appropriate and desirable from the university managers' point of view. Civil servants from the ministry often indirectly refer to values within the representative democracy as arguments for regulating universities, rules that are also referred to by university managers as being too rigid. In other words, sometimes there seems to be a clash between the aims of ensuring democratic rights, which can lead to more process control, and the idea of increasing the university autonomy and removing rules.

The increasing economic resources at the Danish universities seem to influence the governmental regulation. New *problems* are experienced: a demand for securing an appropriate spending of the resources has risen, new problems have emerged with the so-called mass universities, which call for solutions, and problems are observed with the new form of governance, aiming at more outcome control and less process control. For instance, the government has sought to ensure a high quality and relevance in education, student's rights, and an appropriate spending of resources at the universities.

Furthermore, the economic resources are also followed by an increased *interest* for stakeholders and politicians in influencing the university sector. The university domain has become more salient with more students and employees and a higher number of publicly funded resources, which makes the sector increasingly interesting for the Danish voters, politicians, lobbyists, and the Department of Finance. Hence, political executives and stakeholders have a greater interest in influencing the universities.

In line with the literature on rule dynamics, the explanations of why the government's regulation of the universities does not strictly follow the intentions behind the university reforms, why the number of rules in the University Act has increased after 2003, and why the government has reestablished control of both universities' process and output seem to be both interests and problems.

The legal offices and employees are substantial in the Ministry of Higher Education and Research, and as all interviewed civil servants mention in the interviews, it is currently unlikely that the state will govern the Danish universities without using regulation as a policy instrument. Regulation is a well-known instrument, and rules are perceived as effective and efficient means to solve problems and enhance interests. Civil servants do not perceive the development contracts and subsidies as a replacement to rules but as supplementary means of governing the universities.

Conclusion and Discussion

Over the last few decades, the governmental regulation of the Danish universities has changed remarkably. From regulating within a ministerial hierarchy, the ministry has created distance to the universities as the Danish universities' legal status has changed from state institutions to self-governing institutions. Concurrently, the regulation in the ministerial orders has changed to become less specific and less in number. Oppositely, after universities became self-governing institutions in 2003, the government has increasingly regulated universities from a distance through the University Act. In the Act, the government has adopted *both* reform initiatives encompassing rules that have increased university autonomy and managerial authority *and* rules that have increased the governmental control by regulating university educations and stating requirements to the university and university management. As the title of the chapter implies, increased autonomy and authority to decentralized organizations and their managers seem to induce more governmental control.

In overall terms, the analysis of the governmental regulation over time shows a reregulation with an increased number of rules in the Act and a decreased number of rules in the ministerial orders. The government seems to have reestablished their control over the universities as increased university autonomy and authority are followed by increased governmental control. Despite the adoption of university reforms in 1992 and 2003 intending to deregulate the governance of universities and decrease the governmental process control, the Danish government uses the traditional instrument (i.e., rules) to govern the Danish universities throughout the examined period from 1989 to 2015, and they regulate universities' processes.

As indicated in the literature, there has not been a total shift away from a bureaucratic system to a performance management system but rather a layering of different forms of governance. Rationales from both the traditional, rule-based governance and performance management are identified in the governmental regulation of the universities, and rules, contracts, and subsidies are used together in the governance of universities. The interviewed civil servants perceive the policy instruments as complementary, and they perceive the governmental regulation as irreplaceable in the current governance of universities.

In line with the literature on rule dynamics, this study suggests problems and interests as the dynamics behind the rule development and as the overall explanation of the development in the government's regulation of the universities.

A More Nuanced Understanding of a Partial Adoption of Performance Management Reforms

Moynihan has observed performance management reforms to be partially adopted and describes a partial adoption as a lack of increased managerial authority to the decentralized managers (Moynihan 2008: 39–57). Furthermore, Moynihan explains the partial adoption with political executives' attraction to performance management for symbolic—and not instrumental—benefits (Moynihan 2008: 58–74). Political executives' interests in symbolizing "rational" governance but still controlling the decentralized organization is hereby suggested as the explanation of a partial adoption. In other words, Moynihan focuses only on political executives' *interests* as an explanation.

As argued earlier, this description and explanation finds some support in the Danish university case. However, I will argue that this understanding of a partial adoption is too simplified. With inspiration from the literature on rule dynamics, I suggest two overall and supplementary explanations of the partial adoption: *interests* (Jennings et al. 2005; Van Witteloostuijn & de Jong 2007, 2008, 2009) and *problems* (Zhou 1993; Schulz 1998; March et al. 2000).

Moynihan only focuses on political executives' interests, but, in the interviews, civil servants pointed out that also stakeholders and even university managers may be interested in establishing rules regulating the process. Civil servants explain how they have experienced stakeholders from the Danish industry to be interested in having recruitment panels at the universities, which the government have implemented by establishing a process rule in the University Act. University managers may have an interest in process rules for at least two reasons: First, civil servants have experienced that some rules are perceived as necessary to the universities, and it may be more demanding for especially the smaller universities to establish the rules locally than if the rules came from above. Second, it may be more convenient for the university management if unpopular regulation is implemented from the national level. Recruitment rules ensuring that only the best-qualified employees are hired at the university, and not friends, are mentioned by civil servants as an example. They may be perceived as necessary to university managers but unpopular among some employees. When an unpopular regulation comes from above, the universities do not have to spend resources on establishing the rules, and the university managers can possibly "blame" (Hood 2011) the national level for unpopular regulation.

Problems may also be the driver for the partial adoption. Governance by performance management does not always seem usable for governing the universities. It can be difficult to specify goals for universities that are meaningful to all universities, that at the same time are comparable across all Danish universities, that catch all the different aspects of university performance, and that do not have unintended consequences (e.g., Pollitt 2013) or what Dahler-Larsen names "constitutive effects" (Dahler-Larsen 2014). Furthermore, it is difficult to evaluate universities' performance and reward/sanction the good/bad performers: it is difficult to isolate the universities' performance from external factors, and the effects of universities' performance do not appear until after several years.

For instance, a performance indicator such as employment rates succeeds in measuring outcome, but external factors (such as the state of the market) significantly affect the outcome. The university may therefore perform very well under the given circumstances, but because of external factors, the university may still be assessed as a "bad performer". Whether an organization complies with process goals (such as teaching hours) is more directly dependent on the university, but it is not necessarily a good indicator for the quality of the educations.

The challenges of setting targets and evaluating performance are problematic in a performance management system, whereas the government—according to the doctrine of performance management—should set measurable output targets, assess the decentralized organizations' performances, and reward/sanction good/bad performers. If the government cannot evaluate and sanction the universities, it can be difficult to motivate the decentralized managers to accomplish political goals.

Civil servants in the Ministry of Higher Education and Research are skeptical towards governance by performance management, and they find rules to be a necessary tool in order to govern the universities.

> It is not possible to govern without rules, period!
> (Manager, Ministry of Higher Education
> and Research 2016)

> So, it is in combination that it [rules, development contracts, economic incentives] works.
> (Civil servant, Ministry of Higher Education
> and Research 2016)

The government uses regulation, subsidies, and the development contract as supplementary tools, and all the interviewed civil servants also perceive them as such. Governance of the Danish universities by pure performance management seems unrealistic. There are problems in measuring and assessing performance, and stakeholders and university managers seem to be interested in some process rules. Furthermore, political executives also seem to be interested in influencing the universities, as emphasized by Moynihan. When civil servants and politicians do not perceive the new tools and governance strategies as effective as rules to solve problems and enhance interests, civil servants and the government govern in the traditional manner and use a recognizable tool (i.e., regulation).

Overall, there is no simple explanation of a partial adoption of performance management reforms, but, as demonstrated in this section, it may be useful to look at *problems* and *interests* as two overall supplementary explanations.

References

Bemelmans-Videc, M.-L., Rist, R.C. & Vedung, E. 2010, *Carrots, Sticks & Sermons: Policy Instruments and Their Evaluation*, Transaction Publisher, London.

Boyne, G.A. 2010, "Performance Management: Does It Work?" In *Public Management and Performance*, eds. R.M. Walker, G.A. Boyne & G.A. Brewer, The United States of America; Cambridge University Press, New York.

Capano, G. 2011, "Government Continues to Do Its Job. A Comparative Study of Governance Shifts in the Higher Education Sector", *Public Administration*, vol. 89, pp. 1622–1642.

Christensen, T. & Lægreid, P. 2011, "Complexity and Hybrid Public Administration—Theoretical and Empirical Challenges", *A Global Journal*, vol. 11, pp. 407–423.

Christensen, T., Lie, A. & Laegreid, P. 2008, "Beyond New Public Management: Agencification and Regulatory Reform in Norway: Beyond New Public Management", *Financial Accountability & Management*, vol. 24, pp. 15–30.

Dahler-Larsen, P. 2014, "Constitutive Effects of Performance Indicators: Getting Beyond Unintended Consequences", *Public Management Review*, vol. 16, pp. 969–986.

de Boer, H., File, J., Huisman, J., Seeber, M., Vukasovic, M. & Westerheijden, D.F. 2017, "Policy Analysis of Structural Reforms in Higher Education", *Springer Verlag*. www.statsbiblioteket.dk/au/#/search?query=recordID%3A%22summon_FETCH-LOGICAL-c1438-fd87b7f617d01fcc1471b8e013b2dcc3b303bf2745147fd4f026941fb13e89b93%22.

Degn, L. & Sørensen, M. 2015, "From Collegial Governance to Conduct of Conduct: Danish Universities Set Free in the Service of the State", *Higher Education*, vol. 69, pp. 931–946.

Hood, C. 1999, *Regulation Inside Government: Waste-Watchers, Quality Police, and Sleaze-Busters*, Oxford University Press, New York.

Hood, C. 2011, *The Blame Game: Spin, Bureaucracy, and Self-Preservation in Government*, Princeton University Press, Princeton.

Hood, C., James, O., Jones, G., Scott, C. & Travers, T. 1999, *Regulation Inside Government: Waste Watchers, Quality Police, and Sleaze-Busters*, Oxford University Press, Oxford. http://ez.statsbiblioteket.dk:2048/login?url=www. oxfordscholarship.com/view/10.1093/0198280998.001.0001/acprof-978019 8280996; www.statsbiblioteket.dk/au/#/search?query=recordID%3A%22 ebog_ssj0000089230%22.

Jakobsen, M.L.F. & Mortensen, P.B. 2014, *Regelstaten: Væksten I Danske Love Og Bekendtgørelser 1989–2011*. 1. udgave edn, Studier I Offentlig Politik; 1, Jurist- og Økonomforbundets Forlag, Kbh.

Jakobsen, M.L.F. & Mortensen, P.B. 2016, "Rules and the Doctrine of Performance Management", *Public Administration Review*, vol. 76, pp. 302–312.

Jennings, P.D., Schulz, M., Patient, D., Gravel, C. & Yuan, K. 2005, "Weber and Legal Rule Evolution: The Closing of the Iron Cage?", *Organization Studies*, vol. 26, pp. 621–653.

Kulturministeriet, Ministeriet for Videnskab, Teknologi og Udvikling, Velfærdsministeriet, Undervisningsministeriet, Økonomi- og Erhvervsministeriet & Finansministeriet. 2009, "Selvejende Institutioner—Styring, Regulering Og Effektivitet", Finansministeriet, Kbh.

Lægreid, P., Roness, P.G. & Rubecksen, K. 2006, "Performance Management in Practice: The Norwegian Way", *Financial Accountability & Management*, vol. 22, pp. 251–270.

Levitt, B. & March, J.G. 1988, "Organizational Learning", *Annual Review of Sociology*, vol. 14, pp. 319–340.

Maor, M. 1999, "The Paradox of Managerialism", *Public Administration Review*, vol. 59, pp. 5–18.

March, J.G., Schulz, M. & Zhou, H.K. 2000, *The Dynamics of Rules: Change in Written Organizational Codes*, Stanford University Press, Stanford.

Ministry of Science Technology and Innovation. 2009, *The University Evaluation 2009. Evaluation Report*, ed Secondary—. Reprint, Reprint.

Moynihan, D.P. 2005, "Managing for Results in an Impossible Job: Solution or Symbol? Abstract", *International Journal of Public Administration*, vol. 28, pp. 213–231.

Moynihan, D.P. 2008, "The Dynamics of Performance Management: Constructing Information and Reform", in *Public Management and Change Series*, Georgetown University Press, Washington, DC. http://ez.statsbiblioteket.dk:2048/login?url= http://ebookcentral.proquest.com/lib/asb/detail.action?docID=547813; www. statsbiblioteket.dk/au/#/search?query=recordID%3A%22ebog_ssj0000 142107%22.

Olsen, J.P. 2006, "Maybe It Is Time to Rediscover Bureaucracy", *J-PART*, vol. 16, pp. 1–24.

Olsen, J.P. 2007, "The Institutional Dynamics of the European University", in *University Dynamics and European Integration*, eds. P. Maassen & J. P. Olsen, vol. 19, Higher Education Dynamics, Springer, Dordrecht, The Netherlands, pp. 25–54.

Page, E. 2012, *Policy Without Politicians: Bureaucratic Influence in Comparative Perspective*, Oxford University Press, Oxford.

Pollitt, C. 2013, "The Logics of Performance Management", *Evaluation*, vol. 19, pp. 346–363.

Pollitt, C. & Bouckaert, G. 2011, *Public Management Reform: A Comparative Analysis: New Public Management, Governance, and the Neo-Weberian State*, Third edn, Oxford University Press, Oxford.

Schulz, M. 1998, "Limits to Bureaucratic Growth: The Density Dependence of Organizational Rule Births", *Administrative Science Quarterly*, vol. 43, pp. 845–876.

Statsministeriet. 2006, "Regeringens Globaliseringsstrategi. Fremgang, Fornyelse Og Tryghed: Strategi for Danmark i Den Globale Økonomi – de vigtigste initiativer", Regeringen, Schultz Information, Albertslund. http://www.statsminis teriet.dk/multimedia/Fremgang__fornyelse_og_tryghed_.pdf

Uddannelses- og Forskningsministeriet. 2009, "Aftale Om Erasmus Mundus", in *Secondary Aftale Om Erasmus Mundus*, ed Secondary—. Reprint, Reprint. https://ufm.dk/lovstof/politiske-aftaler/aftale-om-erasmus-mundus.pdf

Uddannelses- og Forskningsministeriet. 2013, "Kommissorium. Udvalg for Kvalitet Og Relevans I De Videregående Uddannelser". https://ufm.dk/aktuelt/presse-meddelelser/2013/kvaliteten-af-de-videregaende-uddannelser-skal-loftes/kommissorium_udvalg-for-kvalitet-og-relevans-i-de-videregaende-uddannelser_regeringen-oktober-2013.pdf

Van Witteloostuijn, A. & De Jong, G. 2007, "The Evolution of Higher Education Rules: Evidence for an Ecology of Law", *International Review of Administrative Sciences*, vol. 73, pp. 235–255.

Van Witteloostuijn, A. & De Jong, G. 2008, "Changing National Rules: Theory and Evidence From the Netherlands (1960–2004)", *Public Administration*, vol. 86, pp. 499–522.

Van Witteloostuijn, A. & De Jong, G. 2009, "Ecology of National Rule Birth: A Longitudinal Study of Dutch Higher Education Law, 1960–2004", *Journal of Public Administration Research and Theory*, vol. 20, no. 1, pp. 187–213.

Vedung, E. 2010, "Policy Instrument: Typologies and Theories", in *Carrots, Sticks & Sermons*, Transaction Publisher, New Brunswick.

Zhou, X. 1993, "The Dynamics of Organizational Rules", *American Journal of Sociology*, vol. 98, pp. 1134–1166.

5 Board Influence and Interaction With University Management

Niels Ejersbo and Carsten Greve

Introduction

Many public sector institutions have over the past decade been through reforms of their governance structure. A common feature of these reforms has been an introduction of boards (Hinna, De Nito & Mangia 2010). The introduction of boards is inspired by the governance structure in private companies, where the board of directors is an intermediary between the firm's stakeholders and its top management team (Thomsen & Conyon 2012: 142). In a public sector setting the boards are intermediary between the political level (the relevant ministry) and the management of the public institution. The boards have several roles such as controlling and holding the management accountable, giving advice, acting as representatives or as contact to networks and external actors (Van den Berghe & Levrau 2004; McNulty & Pettigrew 1999; Cornforth 2003). However, we have little knowledge about how the board interacts with other internal actors and how the board influences different levels of the organization. Part of the literature on boards also questions the influence of boards and argues that they are no more than "rubber stamps" (Farrell 2005: 93). Most of the literature and studies on boards concerns private companies, but with an increased use of boards in public sector institutions, we lack knowledge about the functioning and interaction of boards in the public sector. Based on a behavioral approach, this chapter will give new knowledge about the interaction between boards and management at different levels of the organization by addressing the following research questions: *How influential are boards?* and *How do boards interact with management?*

The chapter is structured as follows. In the next section we discuss the influence of boards and present different modes of interaction between boards and management, what influences this interaction, and how different modes of the interaction relates to board influence. The third section describes the data and methods used in the analysis. The penultimate section analyzes board influence and the interaction between university board and management before the concluding section of the chapter.

The Influence of Boards and Modes of Interaction

Boards may take or be given different roles and are expected to fulfill these roles. However, the literature questions the actual influence and importance of boards. Boards are by some considered "ornaments on a corporate Christmas tree" (Bryne 2002 cited in Van den Berghe & Levrau 2004: 461). Management hegemony theory (Farrell 2005) views the board as no more than a "rubber stamp". According to this view, the role of the board is primarily symbolic by giving legitimacy to decisions and actions taken by the management. Thus, boards may not be powerful entities that control and hold the management accountable, interact closely with the management in a pursuit of common objectives, create and link to networks, or effectively represent specific groups or actors. Also in relation to university governance the influence of boards has been questioned (Christensen 2012). Others conclude based on studies of the British health system that the rubber stamp thesis is too crude and somewhat overstated (Ferlie, Pettigrew & Fitzgerald 1996: 163). Although boards are given the formal authority to control, the boards they may lack real authority (Aghion & Tirole 1997).

There is no common understanding on how to measure or understand the influence of boards. Some look at the performance or outcome of the organization. In the private sector this is typically in terms of financial performance (Gabrielsson & Huse 2005: 12). In the public sector success may be more difficult to define, since goals are generally more ambiguous and prioritized differently by numerous shareholders, but they may include public value, legitimacy and support, and operational capabilities (Moore & Hartley 2008). Others point to the influence on selecting/dismissing CEOs (Adams et al. 2008: 12) as a way to capture board influence. Several studies look at strategy and the boards' influence on strategy (see Pugliese et al. for an overview). Formulating the strategy and setting the long-term goals for the organization is one of the main tasks of a board, and measuring board influence by looking at involvement and influence on strategy seems to a relevant approach to measuring board influence. In this chapter, we follow this way for measuring board influence. In addition, we include a second measure. Boards may lack both capabilities and information to get involved or influence the strategy of the organization (Hinna et al. 2010: 148; Rutherford & Buchholtz 2007: 578), and as a consequence it is more or less left to the management to formulate the strategy. Alternatively, specific issues related to the production or service of the organization have the interest of the boards. For boards at educational institutions this could be seeking influence on the recruitment of employees and leaders, study programs, or research areas. Hence, we are also interested in board influence on the content of the production of the institution. In the following analyses, we use three measures of board influence: (1) influence on economy, (2) influence on strategy, and (3) influence on content. The construction of the three measures are described in the data section of the chapter.

Boards can use different methods to interact with other parts of the organization. Boards can be considered the strategic apex of an organization and must as such secure that the mission of the organization is fulfilled in an effective way (Mintzberg 1983: 13). From a principal-agent point of view the board is faced with a control problem vis-á-vis the management and the rest of the organization. The management can have its own objectives that do not necessarily correspond with the goals of the board. Due to information asymmetry between management and the rest of the organization, management has the upper hand and can hide information and actions. In order to handle this problem, the board must find ways to control or influence the management and the rest of the organization. In the following we will look at two different ways that boards can influence the actions of the management and the rest of the organization. One option for the board is to use a bureaucratic mode of interaction using hierarchy and rules to influence the organization. Another option is to use goals, performance contracts, and increased visibility of the management's action. This mode of interaction is inspired by Performance Management and by a New Public Management way thinking.

The board is formally in charge of the organization and can determine the structure and procedures of the organization. They can use their position and authority to set up the ground rules for interaction between the board and the management of the organization. In a bureaucratic mode of interaction, they will rely on a well-established hierarchy where subordinates are controlled by superiors. A bureaucratic organization is, among others, characterized by the principal of fixed and official jurisdictional areas, which are generally ordered by rules; the principles of office hierarchy and levels of graded authority mean a firmly ordered system of super- and subordination in which there is a supervision of the lower offices by the higher ones, and the management of the office follows general rules, which are more less stable, more or less exhaustive, and which can be learned (Hughes 2012: 49; Pollitt 2009).

The use of rules is fundamental to organizing and will be a part of a bureaucratic mode of interaction. March, Schulz and Zhou (2000) discuss the how rules play a very important role in controlling and organizing an organization. Rules can be a way to handle problems of coordination (Peters 1998) and to avoid anarchy (March et al. 2000: 8).

The use of a bureaucratic mode of interaction will be attractive in a university setting. Universities have been given labels such as "academic tribes" (Becher 1989) and organized anarchies (Capano 2011). For the board to get some influence it needs to challenge the academic norms and rules and it needs to implement a more traditional organizational mode of operation. Public organizations are described as incomplete organizations, and many public sector reforms aim at changing them into "real organizations" (Brunsson & Sahlin-Andersson 2000: 722). This is also the case with universities. Transforming public organizations such as universities into real organizations includes setting up hierarchy, changing the modes of managing, controlling, and accounting (Brunsson & Sahlin-Andersson 2000: 722). Thus, we will be expect the bureaucratic mode of interaction to be widely use among university boards.

Performance management is presented as an alternative to hierarchy and bureaucratic rules and procedures (Osborne & Gaebler 1992). It is often presented as a New Public Management–inspired governing instrument (Pollitt & Bouckaert 2011), and has become very popular in the public sector during the past decade. Performance management has been defined in numerus ways, but it include at least that the leadership formulate clear goals and targets (Lægreid, Roness & Rubecksen 2006). A more comprehensive definition is "an integrated set of planning and review procedures which cascade down through the organization to provide a link between the each individual and the overall strategy of the organization" (Rogers cited in Bouckaert & Halligan 2008). It is a management system closely related to strategic steering (Melo, Sarrico & Radnor 2010) and seen as a way to hold the management accountable (Moynihan 2005). Sometimes a system or activity is referred to as performance management without being integrated into the strategy of the organization. Bouckaert and Halling present four models going from preperformance through performance administration, management of performance, and finally performance management. Performance management has also been heavily criticized for not delivering the expected outcomes and for having negative, unintended consequences (Van Thiel & Leeuw 2002; Ohemeng & McCall-Thomas 2013; Rombach 1991; Radin 2012; Van Dooren et al. 2010). When we talk about performance management as a mode of interaction it doesn't necessarily include the full model of performance management (Bouckaert & Halligan 2008). We are especially interested in how the board set up performance results for the university, how the board is involved in the strategy process, and how it makes reference to the performance contract with the ministry.

Performance management is a widespread management tool in public organizations—a popular fashion and organizations gain legitimacy by adopting these types of management tools (Røvik 2007). Hence, we expect the performance management mode of interaction to be widely used among university boards.

Data, Method, and Measures

We sent the web-based questionnaires to all members of the eight Danish university boards and the questionnaire to department heads from

2015. In addition, we use the individual interviews with all chairs of the university boards.

The survey to the board members contained questions concerning their interaction with the rest of the organization and how they prioritized different tasks in order to influence the management and the organization. We have run exploratory factor analysis (principal axis factoring) to validate the factor structure of how the boards interact and try to influence the organization. We find a strong factor for what we have called Hierarchy (loadings around .700), which reflects the board's attempt to control and influence the management through rules and procedures. We also find a second factor reflecting what we have termed Management by Objectives (loadings around .700). It captures how the boards use goals, objectives, and contracts in order to influence the rest of the organization. Based on the factor analysis we have created two indexes. Both indexes have acceptable alpha values—see Table 5.1.

In the survey to department heads we asked questions about their management praxis. Some of the questions focused how they related to the board, if they used the performance contract when making priorities at the department, and if strategies at different levels of the organization were well connected.

We also had a number of questions concerning the department heads' perception of the influence of the boards. How to measure influence is

Table 5.1 Principal axis factoring analyses of latent variables

	M	SD	Factor score	Cronbach's alpha
Mode of interaction				
Hierarchy				.792
• Supervising the university management	2.59	.92	.811	
• Creating suitable frames for control and evaluation of the university management	2.48	.94	.790	
• There are clear rules that the management is expected to follow	2.31	.77	.626	
• The board keeps a tight control with management decisions and actions	2.63	.95	.845	
Management by Objectives				.631
• Preparing the overall strategy of the university	2.02	.88	.633	
• Ensuring that the development contract is met	2.26	.80	.789	
• Determination of internal results for the university and its management	2.37	1.0	.815	

often debated, but we find the perception of the department heads to be a valid measure of the boards influence. Based on factor analysis we have created three indexes to capture different aspects the boards' influence—see Table 5.2. The first index captures how the board influences the budget and the steering of the university's finances and economy (Economy). The second index measures the boards' influence on strategy (Strategy). The third index measures the boards' influence on research areas and choice of studies offered by the university (Content). Taking into account that the indexes each contained two variables, the alpha values are acceptable.

In the analysis of the board influence, we will also look at how the board members evaluate their own influence on economy, strategy, and content.

Due to the multilevel structure of the data, both files were aggregated at the university level and then merged, creating a file with eight cases

First, we look at how department heads and board members assess the influence of the boards. In the second part of the analysis, we use mode of interaction as a dependent variable and look at whether characteristics of the board such as the seniority of board members and the homogeneity within the board (measured as age difference) could explain the choice of interaction. In the third part of the analysis, we look at the relationship between management actions and different modes of interaction and if the mode of interaction is related to the influence of the boards. In other words, we use mode of interaction as the independent variable.

Table 5.2 Principal axis factoring analyses of latent variables

Influence	M	SD	Factor score	Cronbach's alpha
Economy				.781
• Steering the university's economy and finances	1.92	.80	.892	
• The university budget	1.89	.80	.852	
Strategy				.586
• Preparing the university strategy	2.27	.90	.868	
• Realization of the university strategy	3.12	.85	.766	
Content				.536
• Educations offered by the university	3.42	.78	.846	
• Electing the university's research areas	3.63	.97	.786	

Analyzing Board Influence and Board-Management Interaction

In this section, we discuss both how influential the boards actually are and the earlier findings. In the following we first look at how department heads perceive the influence of the boards in three different areas. Second, we see if there is a relationship between the boards' influence and mode of interaction.

The influence of the board in three areas is reported in Table 5.3. The influence of the board clearly depends on the area in question. At all the universities, the board is considered to have a large influence on strategy. The boards are also quite influential at some of the universities when it comes to economy, but there is a much larger variation between the different universities. It comes as no surprise that their influence on research and education (content) is much lower. From the interviews with the chairmen it was very evident that none of them considered it to be an area where the boards should interfere—quite the contrary.

The department heads and the board members evaluation of board influence are quite similar. The largest differences between department heads and board members assessment are in relationship to strategy.

Boards can interact with the university management in different ways. They can use a hierarchical mode of interaction with a focus on rules and procedures or they can set up goals and objectives and interact through a performance management mode of interaction.

Both modes of interaction are used by the university boards—see Table 5.4. The performance management mode of interaction is used more

Table 5.3 Influence of the board

Assessment by department chair and board members index. 100: all answer "Very large influence"; 0: all answer "No influence".

University	Influence on economy		Influence on strategy		Influence on content	
	Dept. chairs	*Board members*	*Dept. chairs*	*Board members*	*Dept. chairs*	*Board members*
KU	74	70	62	63	33	34
CBS	91	85	47	72	30	31
DTU	76	80	67	61	30	36
RUC	83	71	53	70	40	54
SDU	71	68	57	64	44	43
AU	82	75	48	75	35	29
AAU	82	94	65	57	50	31

Note: KU=University of Copenhagen, CBS=Copenhagen Business School, DTU=Technical University of Denmark, RUC=Roskilde University, SDU=University of Southern Denmark, AU=Aarhus University, AAU=Aalborg University

Table 5.4 Mode of interaction

Index: 100: all answer "fully agree/to a very large extent"; 0: all answer "not at all/completely disagree".

University	Hierarchical mode of interaction	Performance management mode of interaction
KU	52.3	67.7
RUC	57.0	70.8
ITU	59.4	70.8
CBS	61.3	70.0
AU	61.3	71.7
SDU	68.1	74.1
AAU	68.8	58.3
DTU	70.5	75.0

Note: KU=University of Copenhagen, CBS=Copenhagen Business School, DTU=Technical University of Denmark, RUC=Roskilde University, SDU=University of Southern Denmark, AU=Aarhus University, AAU=Aalborg University

than the hierarchical mode of interaction at all the universities except for one, but the two modes of interactions are not substitutes for each other. Rather they are clearly used simultaneously. The performance management mode of interaction corresponds well with how the governance system between the Ministry of Research and the universities is designed. As described earlier, the relationship between the ministry and the universities can be described as a performance management system, and there is a performance contract between the ministry and each university to guide the interaction between the ministry and each university. The one exception is AAU where the board relies more on hierarchy and rules than on a performance management mode of interaction. As part of the study we made interviews with all chairmen of the boards. The chair of the AAU board told how the university had been through a difficult period with economic problems. The budget reports had for most of the year shown a deficit of 80 million Danish kroner—twice as much as planned. This was also confirmed at the end of the year. Then one and a half months into the new budget year it turned out that the deficit for the previous year had increased to 180 million. This made the board demand a change in the budget report procedure with monthly reports and requesting more accurate budget reports. This incident occurred before the board members were surveyed may explain why AAU has more focus on the hierarchical mode of interaction.

Following prior research on boards we have used board characteristics as a way to explain the actions of the board. We have looked at the average seniority of the boards and homogeneity in age as the two board characteristics. In Figure 5.1 and Figure 5.2 we report the relationship between average seniority and mode of interaction.

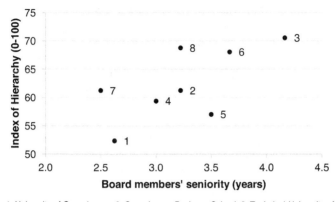

1=University of Copenhagen, 2=Copenhagen Business School, 3=Technical University of Denmark, 4=IT University, 5=Roskilde University, 6=University of Southern Denmark, 7=Aarhus University, 8=Aalborg University

Figure 5.1 The relationship between average seniority of the board members and hierarchical mode of interaction

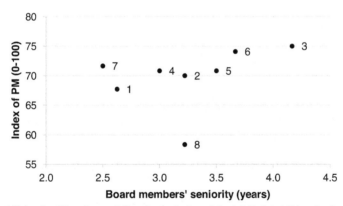

1=University of Copenhagen, 2=Copenhagen Business School, 3=Technical University of Denmark, 4=IT University, 5=Roskilde University, 6=University of Southern Denmark, 7=Aarhus University, 8=Aalborg University

Figure 5.2 The relationship between average seniority of the board members and performance management mode of interaction

It is not possible to establish a clear relationship between board members' seniority and mode of interaction. It looks like there is a tendency for boards with higher seniority to use a hierarchical mode of interaction to a larger extent than boards with lower seniority, but there are also exceptions. We have also analyzed the relationship between the homogeneity of the board (measured as the standard deviation in age) and the mode of interaction (not shown). Again, there is no clear pattern between the two.

In this part of the analysis we first look at how the management reacts to different modes of interaction. We have used three types of measures of management reactions (as expressed by the department heads): (1) When the dean makes demands, he or she uses the board as a reference. (2) There is a connection between the departments' strategy and strategies at other levels of the university. (3) There is a connection between the demands in performance contract and priorities at the department. We only show the figures for the connection between strategies at different levels of the university and mode of interaction—see Figure 5.3 and Figure 5.4. As we can see in Figures 5.3 and 5.4 there doesn't seem to be any clear relationship between mode of interaction and the connection between the strategy of the department and strategies at other levels.

It is the same picture when we look at the other types of reaction from the management (not reported). Based on the findings using the three types of reactions mentioned earlier, it is not possible to establish a clear pattern between the boards' choice of interaction and the reaction from the management.

Finally, we look at the relationship between influence and mode of interaction. We only show the findings in relation to influence on economy (see Figures 5.5 and 5.6). It does not seem to be a clear relationship between influence on economy and mode of interaction.

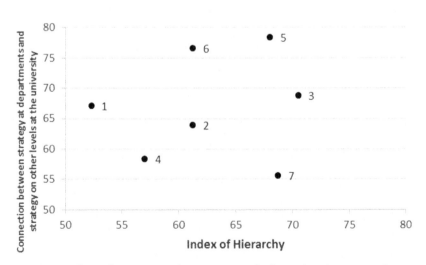

1=University of Copenhagen, 2=Copenhagen Business School, 3=Technical University of Denmark, 4=Roskilde University, 5=University of Southern Denmark, 6=Aarhus University, 7=Aalborg University

Figure 5.3 The relationship between department strategy and strategies at other levels of the organization and hierarchical mode of interaction

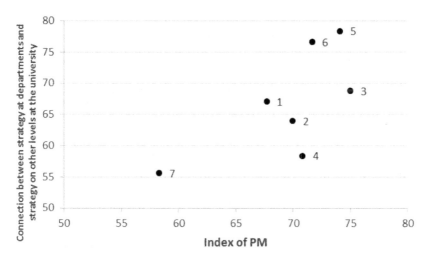

1=University of Copenhagen, 2=Copenhagen Business School, 3=Technical University of Denmark, 4=Roskilde University, 5=University of Southern Denmark, 6=Aarhus University, 7=Aalborg University

Figure 5.4 The relationship between department strategy and strategies at other levels of the organization and performance management mode of interaction

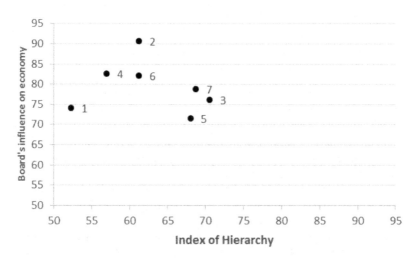

1=University of Copenhagen, 2=Copenhagen Business School, 3=Technical University of Denmark, 4=Roskilde University, 5=University of Southern Denmark, 6=Aarhus University, 7=Aalborg University

Figure 5.5 The relationship between influence on economy and hierarchical mode of interaction

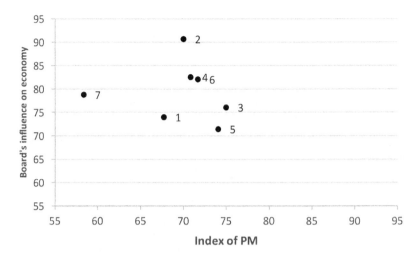

1=University of Copenhagen, 2=Copenhagen Business School, 3=Technical University of Denmark, 4=Roskilde University, 5=University of Southern Denmark, 6=Aarhus University, 7=Aalborg University

Figure 5.6 The relationship between influence on economy and performance management mode of interaction

The same picture holds for the other types of influence (not shown). The influence differs with mode of interaction but in any coherent pattern.

Conclusion

Boards have become an integrated part of governing public organizations and they are used as intermediaries between the political level and the management of the public institutions. Even though boards are used in more and more situations in the public sector we still lack knowledge about board influence and how boards function and how they interact with the rest of the organization.

In this chapter, we look at board influence and two modes of interaction—a hierarchical mode of interaction and a performance management mode of interaction. We argue that both modes of interaction may be relevant for public organizations and especially for universities. Part of the literature on boards is skeptical towards the influence of boards.

The analysis shows that Danish university boards have the most influence on economy and strategy and the least influence on content such as selection of research areas and educations offered by the university. It is also shown that the boards use performance management as a mode of interaction to a larger extent than a hierarchical mode. However, it is also clear that the two modes of interaction are used simultaneously and that there is not necessarily a tradeoff between the two.

We were also interested in links between the mode of interaction and the actions of the university management. However, it was not possible to establish any systematic relationship between the two. The attempt to find systematic patterns between the mode of interaction and type of influence was not successful.

In general, the study has shown how boards interact with management and how the boards' influence differs between areas. However, it has obvious shortcomings when it comes to establishing systematic relationships between the mode of interaction on the one side and management actions and board influence on the other.

References

Adams, R., Hermalin, B. & Weisbach, M. 2008, The Role of Boards of Directors in Corporate Governance: A Conceptual Framework and Survey. *NBER Working Paper Series*. Cambridge, MA: National Bureau of Economic Research.

Aghion, P. & Tirole, J. 1997, "Formal and Real Authority in Organizations", *Journal of Political Economy*, vol. 105, no. 1, pp. 1–29.

Becher, T. 1989, *Academic Tribes and Territories*, Open University Press, Buckingham.

Bouckaert, G. & Halligan, J. 2008, *Performance Management: International Comparisons*, Routledge, New York.

Brunsson, N. & Sahlin-Andersson, K. 2000, "Constructing Organizations: The Example of Public Sector Reform", *Organization Studies*, vol. 21, no. 4, pp. 721–746.

Bryne, J.A. 2002, "Commentary: Boardroom Changes That Could Rebuild Trust", *Business Week*, June 17.

Capano, G. 2011, "Government Continues to Do Its Job: A Comparative Study of Governance Shifts in the Higher Education Sector", *Public Administration*, vol. 89, no. 4, pp. 1622–1642.

Christensen, J.G. 2012, "Magt og management på universiteterne", in *Hvordan styres videnssamfundet? Demokrati, ledelse og organisering*, eds. J.P. Faye & David Budtz, Nyt fra samfundsvidenskaberne, København.

Cornforth, C., ed. 2003, *The Governance of Public and Non-Profit Organisations*, Routledge, Oxon.

Ferlie, E., Pettigrew, A., & Fitzgerald, L. 1996, *The New Public Management in Action*, Oxford University Press, Oxford.

Farrell, C. M. 2005, "Governance in the UK Public Sector: The Involvement of the Governing Board", *Public Administration*, vol. 83, pp. 89–110.

Gabrielsson, J. & Huse, M. 2005, "Outside Directors in SME Boards. A Call for Theoretical Reflections. *Corporate Board*, vol. 1, no. 1, pp. 28–37.

Hinna, A., De Nito, E. & Mangia, G. 2010, "Board of Directors Within Public Organisations: A Literature Review", *International Journal of Business and Ethics*, vol. 5, no. 3, pp. 131–156.

Hughes, O. 2012, *Public Management and Administration. An Introduction.* Basingstoke: Palgrave McMillan.

Lægreid, P., Roness, P.G. & Rubecksen, K. 2006, "Performance Management in Practice: The Norwegian Way", *Financial Accountability & Management*, vol. 22, no. 3, pp. 251–270.

March, J.G., Schulz, M. & Zhou, H.K. 2000, *The Dynamics of Rules: Change in Written Organizational Codes*, Stanford University Press, Stanford.

McNulty, T. & Pettigrew, A. 1999, "Strategists on the Board" *Organization Studies*, vol. 20, no. 1, pp. 47–74.

Melo, A.I., Sarrico, C.S. & Radnor, Z. 2010, "The Influence of Performance Management Systems on Key Actors in Universities", *Public Management Review*, vol. 12, no. 2, pp. 233–254.

Mintzberg, H. 1983, *Structures in Fives*. Englewood Cliffs, NJ: Prentice Hall.

Moore, M. & Hartley, J. 2008, "Innovations in Governance" *Public Management Review*, vol. 10, no. 1, pp. 3–20.

Moynihan, D.P. 2005, "Why and How Do State Governments Adopt and Implement 'Managing for Results' Reforms?" *Journal of Public Administration Research and Theory: J-PART*, vol. 15, no. 2, pp. 219–243.

Ohemeng, F. & McCall-Thomas, E. 2013, "Performance Management and 'Undesirable' Organizational Behaviour: Standardized Testing in Ontario Schools", *Canadian Public Administration*, vol. 56, no. 3, pp. 456–477.

Osborne, D.E. & Gaebler, T. 1992, *Reinventing Government*, Plume, New York.

Peters, B.G. 1998, "Managing Horizontal Government: The Politics of Co-Ordination", *Public Administration*, vol. 76, no. 2, pp. 295–311.

Pollitt, C. 2009, "Pathologies of the Neo-liberal State: From Bureaucracy to Framnetocracy?", *Norsk Statsvitenskapelig Tidsskrift*, vol. 25, pp. 160–182.

Pollitt, C. & Bouckaert, G. eds. 2011, *Public Management Reform*, Third edn. Oxford: Oxford University Press.

Radin, B. 2012, *Federal Management Reform in a World of Contradictions*, CQ Press, Washington, DC.

Rombach, B. 1991, *Det går inte att styra med mål*, Studentlitteratur, Lund.

Røvik, K.A. 2007, *Trender og translasjoner: Idéer som former det 21. århundredes organisation*. Oslo: Universitetsforlaget.

Rutherford, M.A. & Buchholtz, A.K. 2007, "Investigating the Relationship Between Board Characteristics and Board Information", *Corporate Governance: An International Review*, vol. 15, pp. 576–584.

Thiel, S.V. & Leeuw, F.L. 2002, "The Performance Paradox in the Public Sector", *Public Performance & Management Review*, vol. 25, no. 3, pp. 267–281.

Thomsen, S. & Conyon, M. 2012, *Corporate Governance*, Djøf Publishing, Copenhagen.

Van Den Berghe, L.A.A. & Levrau, A. 2004, "Evaluating Boards of Directors: What Constitutes a Good Corporate Board?", *Corporate Governance*, vol. 12, no. 4, pp. 461–478.

Van Dooren, W., Bouckaert, G. & Halligan, J. 2010, *Performance Management in the Public Sector*. London: Routledge.

6 Department Chairs—Modern Managers or Old Administrators?

Niels Ejersbo and Carsten Greve

Public sector management has been through tremendous changes over the past decades (Christensen & Lægreid 2011). The role has changed from a focus on administration and rule-following to a modern manager that develops strategies, using performance information and modern technics to motivate employees. The question is how this development has influenced the department chairs. The chapter looks at how the role of department chair has changed, the recruitment of department chairs, their view on career opportunities, the management role of the department chair, and their view on management challenges.

Changes for Public Managers in Paradigms in Public Governance

The last decades have seen a change in the way public management reform is viewed, and consequently changes are also present in the roles public managers are expected to perform.

The first modern wave of reform is generally known as New Public Management (NPM) reform (Hood 1991). These reforms were aimed at improving public managers' capabilities of being managers like in the private sector and focus on strategy and outputs. While the first part of the NPM prescription elevated the status of management as a discipline, including performance management, the second part of the NPM prescription called for market-type mechanisms to be installed across many public services, including education and higher education. NPM was originally a reaction against a closed Weberian bureaucracy, and NPM could put pressure on a closed bureaucracy by letting citizens act as customers in a quasi-market for public services delivery. A consequence of the NPM idea has been that evaluators, accountants, regulators, and other overseers have to check if the performance is akin to what was promised in the contracts and the performance plans. NPM has therefore often been associated with regulation and control in the "audit society" as Michael Power (1997) talked about. For many, NPM has become equal to "excessive" control and box-ticking as a supplement to the original idea of more management and markets.

When the NPM idea (but not the practice) ran out of steam, the public sector got more preoccupied with how organizations could collaborate and cooperate in networks across organizational boundaries. This approach took up a long-standing tradition in the social sciences for interorganizational collaboration and networks. The trend was linked with various labels, and perhaps "network governance" (Klijn & Koppenjan 2016) or "the New Public Governance" (Osborne 2010) were the ones that were most memorable. In this line of thought, organizations address "wicked problems" that are too complex to solve by any one organization alone, and organizations, including universities, are likely to collaborate on a number of issues if they want to press ahead with their strategies.

Sensing a wider distribution of management authority, and an increased focus on a variety of networks instead of the traditional state focus, a recent trend in the literature on public management reform has been to rethink the contributions by Weber, and to hold on the customer orientation and the performance focus associated with NPM. The label has become known as the Neo-Weberian State (NWS) model and described by Pollitt and Bouckaert (2017) in their latest book on public management reform. The idea is that the state claws back some of the powers that were distributed in network and reassert more central coordination powers again. The state builds upon performance management to ensure that the centrally set targets are met, and the state also aims to deliver more targeted services to appease customers.

The role of public managers, while retaining some core elements on handling resources efficiently, setting targets, motivating employees, and providing some sort of strategic direction, changes according to the substance of the public governance paradigm that is in operation.

The NPM manager is mostly associated with what many people see as agreed tasks for any public manager nowadays: Managers must focus on performance targets and master performance management techniques. Managers should build incentives for their employees and for the organizations that work for them. And managers contract out some of the work to other organizations, either through contracting out with private providers or nonprofit organizations, or with other public organizations in internal partnerships. NPM managers are also aware that citizens-as-customers may change preferences in terms of providers, so NPM managers are keen to provide competitive services that cater to the needs of the customers. NPM managers are generally seen as operating in a quasi-marketplace where there are other organizations/competitors that offer the same kind of service so there is a fierce competition on price/quality of the particular services.

The NPG manager is more focused on collaboration and partnerships with other organizations, and on how to achieve common goals with a diverse set of actors. The first thing on the NPG manager's mind is therefore not competition but cooperation and seeking how possibilities of how to connect with other like-minded organizations. The management and leadership style associated with NPG has been described at length in the literature on networks and governance by Klijn and Koppenjan (2016) and others, but is perhaps nowhere better phrased than in Bryson and Crosby's title on "Leadership for the common good in shared-power world". A recent move in this literature is the focus on public value governance (Page, Stone, Bryson & Crosby 2015), which takes up the gauntlet from Mark Moore and the idea of creating public value and extends to a network setting where public value can only be achieved by an elaborate process where many managers from many organizations work together.

The NWS manager is focused on a select number of tasks: setting performance targets and coordinating (at the center), seeing to it that citizens (as both citizens and citizens-as-customers) are happy with the service or treatment they are getting, and making sure the policy implementation runs smoothly and effectively. Effective implementation is perhaps the most vital part of the NWS manager's job description. The NWS manager recognizes that he or she is a smaller cog in a large machinery, and the job is to get the policy implemented to the satisfaction of the elected politicians and the top public executive in the ministries. The NWS resembles the classic civil servant in many ways, but is more concerned with central coordination and implementation that mere rule following. The NWS manager is a return to the Weberian focus on being a guardian for the state and taking the long view of what is in the state's interest as a state (Byrkjeflot, Du Gay & Greve 2018).

The Focus on Management in Universities

The literature on the role of managers in universities has clear traces of the discussed debate on the public governance paradigms and the various roles for managers.

Better Management

The focus on "better management" and more streamlined management processes also at universities actually goes back a long time, and predates NPM by several decades. Thorstein Veblen (1918) had already written about introducing business administration techniques in academia. Veblen was talking about a centralized plan that would make university administration more rational and in line with the best business practices of the day. "The management revolution" of the universities was heralded by

Rourke and Brookes (1966) in the 1960s. They called for a strengthening of management positions in universities. Amaral et al. (2003) echoed the management focus, with a call for a "higher education management revolution". Amaral has shown how Europe, Canada, Australia, and New Zealand were in the midst of the "management era". The transformation of the public sector into a more restricted and managed sector was also identified in higher education (Paradeise 2009). A specific interest in management teams has also been present in this literature: or, like it is often called "the executive committee" or "senior management"—which consists of the head of the organization (e.g., rector, president, vice-chancellor) and deputy leaders (Sporn in Forest & Altbach 2007: 148). Locke and Bennion (2011) sees a clear shift in power from academic councils to standing committees chaired by university managers. This is clearly in line with NPM's focus on strong managers and strong management teams that can set a strategic direction of an organization. Sporn (2001) examines a trend towards more adaptive universities where the focus on governance, management and leadership is needed to be able to respond to outside pressures. The increasing focus on management also often leads to an increasing focus on leadership and the need for strong leadership capabilities at the very top of a university's hierarchy. Bozeman et al. (2013) finds that the department head authority can be preserved under certain conditions. Bozeman shows that increasing power is related to external hiring, being male, and with department size. Bozeman and colleagues developed a "power index" to measure the autonomy of the department head. The power index shows that a strategic priority of research is beneficial to retaining a degree of autonomy as a department head. Cheng has conducted a study of how performance-based pay is related to performance. Although Cheng's data concerns university presidents and not department heads, Cheng shows that performance-based pay does not play a big role in university presidents' remuneration, and in fact the payment structure resembles that of an ordinary bureaucrat.

More Management, but Also More Control?

A key criticism both in scholarly work, but also in the public sphere, has been that NPM leads to more evaluation and control. There is a dearth of critical literature that thinks that the management trend has gone far, and that the managerial revolution tends to lead to more administration and bureaucracy, and more evaluation, regulation, and control. This is in line with the criticism leveled at the NPM idea mentioned previously. There was already talk of "the bureaucratization of the universities" in 1998 (Gornitzka et al., 1998) and researchers in higher education studies have since foretold the "fall of the faculty and the rise of the all-administrative university" (Ginsberg 2011). Ginsberg criticizes an explosive growth in administration and a decline in the influence of faculty power in U.S.

universities. The relationship between managers and leaders vis-á-vis the faculty have seen some major shifts in the managers and leaders' favour (Clark 2003; Gumport & Pusser 1999; Marginson & Considine 2000; Sporn 2001). In Europe, the delegation of authority to the organizational level has meant the need to increase capacity to manage and lead the university. In the U.S., this trend has been in place for many decades, and the capacity of administration shows in its size (often twice that of faculty). In general, leaders, managers and administrators gained more authority in speaking and deciding for the universities (Sporn in Forest and Altbach 2007: 151). Using an "institutional logics" perspective, Blaschke et al. (2014) finds that the trend towards NPM in universities is not so clear cut. He and his coauthors report from a longitudinal study of a university in Germany, and the article finds that organizational change unfolds in four complementary micro patterns, and that it is not the case the NPM simply replaces collegialism. Blaschke and his colleagues find that decision authority on strategic issues still resides with the university despite the increase in external control measures.

Towards a New Public Governance Type of University Management?

An alternative view to the more management and NPM-focused studies of the universities is provided by Frost et al. (2016) in their book on *Multi-Level Governance in Universities*. Frost and colleagues go back to the key insights from organization theory, and do not only look at the internal management relations of a university, but instead look at how universities craft strategies to cope with expectations and demands from the external environment and form their structure accordingly. In this approach, universities come forward as highly complex organizations with equally highly complex technical and institutional environments, and therefore universities' governance strategies need to be suited to the pressures from both inside the organization as well as outside the organization. This resembles the wider governance perspective that is so prevalent in public management and public administration studies where organizations are seen as managing uncertainty and being part of governing networks (Klijn & Koppenjan 2016). Frølich et al. (2013) also see universities as organizations that navigate in institutional pluralism and focus their practical strategies on coping with conflicting external demands, trying to conduct sense-making in Weick's meaning of the concept to steer the organization through uncertainty. Frølich et al. examine how university managers deal with complexity in strategic activities. Frølich et al. uses a strategy-in-practice perspective, which is an acknowledged strand of research in strategy studies. Salter and Tapper (2013) also focus on the volatile external environment of the universities, and argue that these external pressures influence the internal organization of universities. This is also an organization theory contingency view about finding the right fit between strategy and environment.

Summing up: Management and Governance in the Literature on Change in Universities

The brief insight into some of the recurring themes in the recent literature on management and governance in universities has shown the following: There seems to be a widespread acknowledgment of the profound influence that NPM (or managerialism) has had on managing in the university sector. This view on NPM's effects echoes the wider literature on public sector organizations, which has for several decades now been preoccupied with how NPM changes institutions. The writings on management in the universities seem to be dominated by the way that better management has been promoted and with the intended and unintended consequences that NPM brings with it. Many studies are also engaged in criticizing the turn to NPM and see the evaluation and control theme as being present because of NPM. Other studies are more focused on how universities can develop strategies that help them create value in a volatile environment. The external pressures on universities are strong, and strategies are need by university managers to cope with the changes. A growing number of studies are interested in the universities as part of a wider network governance structure and where department heads become network managers that deal with uncertainty. There does not seem to be many studies yet that associate university management with the NWS governance paradigm yet.

Data, Methods, and Measures

In this chapter, we use data from two surveys with department chairs at Danish universities. The one survey is conducted 2011 and the second in 2015. Some of the questions in the two surveys are identical, which makes it possible to register possible developments between the times of the two surveys. We also report findings from questions only used in one of the surveys. In addition, we draw on qualitative interviews with department chairs carried out in 2010 and 2011. In Chapter 2, we describe data and methods more extensively. Later, we give an account for the variables constructed to this chapter.

We have run exploratory factor analysis (principal axis factoring) to validate the factor structure of how department chairs give priority to different management tasks. Based on the factor analysis we have created four indexes: (1) culture and common values, (2) decision-making, (3) economy and efficiency, and (4) external relations with strong factor loadings. All four indexes have acceptable alpha values—see Table 6.1.

In both surveys (2011 and 2015), we asked question about conditions that had a negative impact on the possibility for the department chair to

Table 6.1 Principal axis factoring analyses of latent variables; managerial tasks, 2011 survey

Leadership tasks	M	SD	Factor score	Cronbach's alpha
Culture and common values				.735
Creating and maintaining a well-defined culture that everyone shares			.694	
Signaling which goals and values I stand for as head of department			.625	
Ensuring that the institute has a reputation in the outside world that makes employees proud			.607	
Creating traditions and stories that bind the institute together			.709	
Creating a common understanding of what is the department's mission			.634	
Decision-making				
Securing compromise in situations where there are conflicts of interest between people or groups at the institute			.435	
Ensuring that the individual employee receives feedback and recognition			.601	
Ensuring that there is a broad acceptance of the key decisions of the institute			.779	
Ensuring that the powerful employees back up my course of action			.498	
Being informed about the employee's views			.740	
Economy and efficiency				.647
Ensuring that the department's resources are used as efficiently as possible			.748	
Ensuring that the department has clear goals and a strategy for how the goals are achieved			.488	
Ensuring that the department is organized with a clear structure and sensible division of labor			.682	
Ensuring ongoing monitoring of the department's finances			.626	
External relations				.546
Managing the institute's interests in relation to the faculty			.800	
Securing resources from the environment, such as the faculty, the university, foundations, companies etc.			.709	

carry out his or her job. We ran a factor analysis and find three strong factors for what we call economic and external requirements, internal conflicts, and hierarchical conflicts. We then constructed three indexes to capture the main challenges. The three indexes have acceptable alpha values when the low number of variables included in the indexes are taken into account—see Table 6.2.

Table 6.2 Principal axis factoring analyses of latent variables

Challenges as department chair	M	SD	Factor score	Cronbach's alpha
Economic and external requirements				.559
New state requirements and rules			.862	
Financial problems at the department			.722	
Internal conflicts				.706
Conflicts of interest between departments/groups at the department			.820	
Personal conflicts among the department's employees			.880	
Hierarchical conflicts				.624
Conflicts between institute and faculty			.773	
Demands from the university's management for administrative procedures at the department			.580	
Unclear signals from the dean/rector			.838	

Department Chairs as Managers

In the following, we analyze the recruitment of department chairs, their view on career opportunities, the management role of the department chair, the use of management instruments, and their view on management challenges.

The Danish University Law from 2003 changed the recruitment to academic leadership positions at the universities in Denmark. Prior to the change in legislation faculty at the university elected the rector, deans, and department chairs. After the change, a board with external majority appointed the rector, which appointed the deans, which again appointed the department chairs. The appointments were usually for a five-year period with the possibility for a three-year extension. After that period, the university had to initiate a new and open recruitment process. This opened the academic leadership positions for people outside the university and the possibility for market for academic leaders. The changes in the recruitment process at the Danish universities followed a common trend in the public sector with more emphasis on leadership qualifications and less on knowledge of the specific organization/sector. There were, however, still some requirements for the applicants. For departments chairs, the applicant must be "a recognized researcher and must have experience in the educational field to the relevant extent" (The Danish Act on Universities, §14,4, 2011). This excludes the vast majority of possible applicants from outside the university sector.

As shown in Table 6.3, about two-thirds of department heads are recruited from within the department and the number has increased

Table 6.3 Background of department chairs, 2011 and 2015

	Employed at the department before becoming department chair	Employed outside the department before becoming department chair
2011	67%	33%
2015	69%	31%
Respondents that only took part in the 2015 survey	72%	28%

Table 6.4 Leadership education among department chairs, 2011

Leadership education (2011)	Percentage (N: 129)
No leadership education	12
Master's degree in leadership/management	6
Diploma degree in leadership/management	1
Department chair program	50
Shorter external courses/program	36
Shorter internal courses/program	40

slightly from 2011 to 2015. If we look at the respondents that only took part in the 2015 survey, the increase is larger.

The opening of a market for academic leadership positions at the department level has not taken place. However, there are examples recruitments from outside the university/department, but this has mostly been at rectors and deans.

A motive behind the introduction of appointed instead of elected leaders was to improve the quality of academic leaders. The position as department head should no longer by occupied by senior faculty members taking their turn, but by someone with leadership skills and who is possibly making a career as an academic leader. Hence, it is interesting to see whether department chairs have leadership experience, have taken formal leadership training, and see themselves as leaders—as opposed to academics.

Among the department chairs in 2011 very few had a formal leadership degree. Half of them had taken part in a specific department chair program offered by University of Southern Denmark and supported by Danish Universities (the association of universities in Denmark). A little more than one-third participated in shorter internal or external leadership training courses while 12 percent had no leadership education.

Even thou only a few have formal leadership training in terms of master's degrees a very large majority have some kind of leadership training. The department chair program does not qualify as formal education, but

Table 6.5 The department chairs' views on career opportunities, 2011 and 2015 (percent)

	2011 (N: 129)	2015 (N: 92)
I am a primarily a researcher, but I am the head of department for a few years and then continue my research career	20.0	19.6
It is unclear whether I want to make a career as a leader or return to a research position	33.6	29.3
I expect to continue as head of department at my current institute - maybe even for the rest of my career	17.6	30.4
I will certainly continue in university management	8.0	9.8
I am a primarily a leader and will certainly continue as a leader—either in the research world or elsewhere	20.8	10.9
Total	100	100

it gave the participants theoretical insight as well as practical leadership training. It is fair to say that, already in 2011, the department chairs had at least some leadership training. The question is whether we can locate a clear leader-identity among the department chairs. We have asked them how they see their future career. This can give us some indication as how they view the position as department chair and their commitment to the leadership role. A first indication is whether they have a guaranteed faculty position when the finish their term as department chair. In 2011, 90 percent of the department chairs have a guaranteed faculty position at the end of their term. Of those without a guaranteed position, almost all were recruited outside the department.

In Table 6.5, we report how the department chairs see their career opportunities in 2011 and 2015. The proportion that either see themselves primarily as researchers or are undecided whether they want to continue as leader or return to research are stable across the two periods.

What is more interesting is the change in the proportion that expect to continue as department heads, possibly for a longer period of time, and those that primarily see themselves as leaders. The first group has increased while the other group has decreased. These changes may indicate that there is a stronger identification as department chairs but not necessarily as leaders in general. All in all, among the department chairs there is an identity as managers and the status of management at the universities has been elevated.

Leadership and Management Roles

The different management concepts send many expectations on leaders and managers in public organizations, and they must be able to handle numerous roles and tasks. This also seem to be the case with department chairs. Looking at the four different leadership roles it is evident that they all cover important tasks for department chairs (see Table 6.6). Representing the department and attracting funding externally is the most important role for department chairs at Danish universities. We can elaborate this role by drawing on the qualitative interviews. One key element in this role is to shield the employees from all sorts of demands—both from outside the university but also from the university administration. The department chairs handle administrative tasks, economy, and other demands on faculty, giving them time to do research and teach. A second element closely related is handling "university politics" vis-á-vis the dean. The department chair must, on the one hand, manage department affairs and protect the department from outside risk and, on the other hand, be able to take part in the overall running of the school in collaboration with the dean. This is clearly not an easy role to fulfill and the dual loyalty can be the basis for many conflicts. A third element relates to representing the department in relation to external actors—with special emphasis on attracting external funding.

It is also evident that handling economic affairs and setting goals and strategies for the department is considered an important role. There are differences in how much economic autonomy departments have vis-á-vis the school/dean. In some cases, the economic situation of the department is almost entirely dependent upon number of students passing exams, faculty publication, and external funding. In other cases, the majority of the economy is in the hands of the dean who then distributes resources to the department dependent upon on a combination of objective measures, tradition, and negotiations between the dean and the department chair. The former case illustrates a management scheme inspired by New Public Management, where use of economic incentives and a high level of decentralization are key factors. Formulating strategies and setting goals for the activities at the department have become a key element for department chairs—90 percent of the departments in the survey have a written strategy. We discuss the use of strategies more thoroughly in a later section.

The department chairs emphasize the roles related to creating a common culture and decision-making and support less than the two roles

Table 6.6 The weight of different leadership roles; assessment by department chairs, 2011 survey

Role	Department chair	N
Representation and external funding	83	129
Economy and strategy	80	129
Creating a common culture at the department	74	129
Decision-making and support	70	129

Index: 100: all answer "Very large weight"; 0: all answer "No weight".

discussed previously, but they are clearly still important roles. The importance of creating a common culture at the department shows that running a department is not just a question of handling administrative matters and economy. The department chairs take on a leadership role trying to formulate narratives and establish traditions that will create stronger ties to the department. This is also an illustration of the stronger leadership identity among department chairs. In addition, working towards a common culture illustrates how universities slowly are moving towards "real organizations" (Brunsson & Sahlin-Anderson 2000; Brunsson 2013). It is an attempt to make departments consist not just of individual researchers that happen to share a common workplace (office hotel), but instead create a unit that are working towards common goals and share the mission of the department. The role related to decision-making and support is the least prioritized role—even though it still is a role of importance. It is important for the department chair to have support for central decision-making in order to run the department and to avoid too many conflicts. Likewise, the department chairs attach weight to having support from the entire organization when making decisions.

We have also run regression analyses looking for factors that may explain some of the variation in the weight put on different roles (not shown). We have looked at personal characteristics of the department chair (age, gender, seniority as department chair, master's degree in management/ leadership), academic fields (Humanities, Health, Social science, Science, and Technology), and the economic situation at the department. However, none of the variables could explain variation across all the four roles. Academic field, gender, and seniority were important in relation to one or two of the roles but not to all. Furthermore, we could not find any significant relation between leadership role and the economic situation of the department or whether the department chair had formal management/leadership training.

The analyses show that several of the management paradigms mentioned in the beginning of the chapter influence department chairs at universities in Denmark. Strategy and setting goals for the department is usually associated with New Public Management, while the concern with representing the department outside actors and creating alliances to handle pressure relates to New Public Governance. The acknowledgement of their dependence on the entire organization show the influence from the New Weberian state paradigm.

Strategy

If we are measuring universities attempt to become "real organizations" by the use of strategies at departments, we have a clear-cut case—90 percent of the departments have a written strategy. According to the survey data (see Table 6.7), the strategy is also well connected to strategies at

Table 6.7 Reactions to statements about the department's strategy, those who answered "to a high/very high degree" (percent)

Statement about the strategy	To a high/very high degree Percent (N: 99)
The strategy contains some clear objectives for the department	84
The strategy is used internally at the department	72
The strategy is used in communication with university management	62
The strategy is used in communication with external parties outside the university	37
The department has a strategy because it is expected from above	16
I regularly use the strategy when making decisions	59
There is a connection between the department's strategy and strategies at other levels of the university	67
The strategy has primarily symbolic meaning	6

other levels of the organization. The extensive use of strategies at department is also a sign of a managerial approach to running a department. Strategies are traditionally associated with the private sector, but the New Public Management paradigm has made use of strategies common in public sector institutions as well. Even though universities are becoming more "market-like" (Berman 2012), the survey data and the qualitative interviews with department chairs show that the institutional setting and the local context influence use of strategies at university department. Strategies are not symbolic—they influence decision-making and priorities but not in an instrumental way. As shown in Table 6.7, a very large majority of the departments chairs report that the strategies include clear objectives. This is in line with the New Public Management recipe where performance targets and "must-win-Battles" is an integrated part of formulating strategies. When talking to the department chairs about the strategies it becomes clear that the objectives in the strategies do not necessarily concern the content or output of the research at the department. It is more an attempt to outline a direction for the activities at the department or to put forward principals that can be used as guidelines. Examples mentioned in the interviews show that strategies wish to connect research and teaching closer, to emphasize the importance of research collaboration between different parts of the department, or to highlight that research must be relevant to society. Strategies are also used to handle local challenges such as integrating a department after an amalgamation.

The department chairs use strategies internally at the department, when they are making decisions, and as a way to communicate to the higher levels at the university. They use it to make a better correspondence between the department's objectives and the goals of the individual researcher. It can also be a way to make groups of researchers formulate common objectives in order to set a direction for their research. This is closely connected to the attempts to create a common culture at the department mentioned earlier. However, it is a general comment across the interviews that research ideas and the development of research starts with the individual researcher. According to most of the department chairs in the qualitative interviews, their strategies point out a direction or set general principals but must not overlook the importance of the individual researcher. Some of them are very articulate about the need to strike a balance between the use of strategies to set a common direction for the department and to give researchers freedom to develop and pursue novel research ideas.

The use of strategies at university departments illustrate very well how universities are influenced by new managerial trends and recipes, but at the same time it has specific institutional characteristics that translate or modify the use of specific tools. The departments have adopted strategies and at the same time are department chairs very much aware of the limitations and potential conflict related to the use of strategies.

Challenges for Department Chairs

Universities have been through major reforms and they are subject to an increasing political interest. For some they are the solution to future challenges in society. The general view of the role of universities has also changed. Universities are no longer just a "community of scholars" but should also actively engage with society and compete for resources on a market basis. In addition, the form of governance for the Danish universities has been through major changes that call for a new role for department chairs. Against this backdrop, it is relevant to investigate some of the challenges department chairs face as part of their job. We asked in 2011 and again in 2015 about some typical challenges for department chairs. Based on their answers, we constructed three indexes (the construction of the indexes is described previously), which are displayed in Table 6.8.

The most common challenge relates to economy and external matters, and the department chairs find this more challenging in 2015 than in 2011. It is especially the rules and requirements from the state that department chairs find frustrating. The many rules from the state and examples of micromanagement are both critiques also mentioned by chairmen of the university boards (see Chapter 5) and can be found across the university sector. Department chairs are especially exposed to rules related to teaching and the running of study programs. There have been several attempts across the public sector in Denmark to cut red tape,

Table 6.8 Conditions that have had a negative impact on the possibility to carry out the job as department chair, 2011 and 2015

Challenges		N	Mean	Std. deviation
2011	Economy and external requirements	128	47	25.00
	Internal conflicts	128	30	22.58
	Hierarchical conflicts	128	37	19.06
2015	Economic and external requirements	98	57	24.49
	Internal conflicts	98	28	19.54
	Hierarchical conflicts	98	32	20.85

Index: 100: all answer "To a very high degree"; 0: all answer "Not at all".

but it has clearly not had any influence on the experiences of the department chairs. There are also challenges related to the economic situation at the department. It can be a consequence of reduced state funding to higher education in general and increased pressure to find external funding to finance research.

Challenges related to internal conflicts and hierarchical conflicts have to a lesser extent had a negative impact on the job as department chair. Hierarchical conflicts relate to demands from upper levels at the university management to administrative procedures. There has been an increased focus on the cost of university administration and there have been reports documenting substantial differences in administrative costs across Danish universities (PricewaterhouseCoopers 2011). This has given upper level management a reason to evaluate local procedures and to streamline procedures in order to cut administrative expenses. Furthermore, more attention on documentation and quality assurance programs result in more control from upper level management.

Interestingly, internal conflicts do not seem to have had a negative impact on the possibilities for the department heads to carry out their job. To sum up: despite the many reforms and a new form of governance, the department chairs do not seem to experience major challenges inside the universities. Most challenges relate to rules and requirements from the state.

Conclusion

The role of leaders of public institutions have changed over the past decades. New governance paradigms introduced specific recipes for good leadership and which management tools to use. Inspired by the private sector, New Public Management gave public leaders an independent and privileged role. They were no longer just a colleague with a special task or the one with most professional knowledge. Universities have been "slow movers", but the changes in the rest of the public sector have also influenced the universities. In the beginning of the chapter, we asked how this development has influenced the department chairs.

The new University Act changed the governance structure at Danish universities and introduced appointed leaders instead of elected leaders. This opened up the door for candidates from outside the university/ department. The analyses show that department chairs for the most part are recruited from inside the department. There is not a large market for department chairs that move between universities or related departments. However, we find signs of a "leader-identity" as department chairs. A growing number of the surveyed department chairs see a future career as department chairs at their current department.

We can also see how the different governance paradigms have influenced the department chairs. They have not become "New Public Management" or "New Public Governance" department chairs. Rather, we trace all of the latest governance paradigms and we ask them about leadership roles, their use of strategy, and their management challenges. Department chairs set targets and goals for their departments, and they formulate strategies as prescribed by New Public Management. The analyses of strategy use also show us that department chairs do not use an instrumental manner, but they adapt to the institutional characteristics of a research environment. Likewise, a New Public Governance perspective is visible with department chairs' focus on representing the department and emphasis on collaboration with actors outside the university/ department. As pointed out by Bryson and Crosby (1992) they operate in a "shared power world" where creating partnerships is critical for development and handling challenges. In a New Weberian State paradigm, the state/center has regained some of its power. When we ask department chairs about challenges, they mention rules and requirements from the state as the biggest (and increasing) challenge. They must be able to operate in a setting where the state increasingly interferes and sets demands. On the organizational level, department chairs must balance between what serves the department and loyalty to the dean/upper-level management. The new University Act created a formal hierarchy, and the department chair must observe the ground rules in a hierarchy.

It has been pointed out that universities are complex organizations in a multifaceted institutional environment. In order to handle the complexity, department chairs observe and select perspectives, mechanisms and tools from the different governance paradigms available. This can be a way for department chairs to function as leaders between strong institutional norms and values, increased political interests, and changing views on the role of the university.

References

Bryson, J. & Crosby, B. 1992, *Leadership for the Common Good*, Jossey-Bass, San Francisco.

Byrkjeflot, H., du Gay, P. & Greve, C. 2018, "What Is the 'Neo-Weberian State' as a Regime of Public Administration?", in *The Palgrave Handbook of Public*

Administration and Management in Europe, eds. É. Ongaro, S.v. Thiel, Palgrave Macmillan, London, pp. 991–1009.

Christensen, T. & Lægreid, P. 2011, *The Ashgate Companion to the New Public Management*, Ashgate, Aldershot.

Hood, C. 1991, "A Public Management for All Seasons?", *Public Administration*, vol. 69, no. 1, pp. 3–19.

Klijn, E.-H. & Koppenjan, J. 2016, *Governance Networks in the Public Sector*, Routledge, London.

Osborne, S. ed. 2010, *The New Public Governance?* Routledge, London.

Page, S., Stone, M., Bryson, J. & Crosby, B. 2015, "Public Value Creation by Cross-Sector Collaborations: A Framework and Challenge of Assessment", *Public Administration*, vol. 93, vol. 4, pp. 715–732.

Pollitt, C. & Bouckaert, G. 2017, *Public Management Reform*, 4th edn. Oxford University Press, Oxford.

Power, M. 1997, *The Audit Society*, Oxford University Press, London and Oxford.

7 Autonomy and Performance Contracts at Universities

Niels Ejersbo, Signe Pihl-Thingvad, and Maiken K. Westergaard

Introduction

Governance in higher education has undergone significant changes in the recent decades (Bleiklie & Kogan 2007). Some countries have made a shift toward a greater decentralization with increased institutional autonomy while other countries have done the opposite (Capano 2011: 1622). However, broader public sector reforms in most Western countries have increased focus on performance in the last three decades (Rainey 2009; Kettl 2000), and performance management (PM) has become a prominent management strategy within the public sector (Moynihan 2008; Pollitt & Bouckaert 2017). This tendency is also reflected in higher education governance, and in many Western countries higher education is governed through a steering-at-a-distance approach (Capano 2011: 1627; Christensen & Lægreid 2007), which includes a focus on performance (results and outcomes) and increased organizational autonomy at the local level—at least ideally (Degn & Sørensen 2015; Enders, de Boer & Weyer 2013; Christensen 2010; Bleiklie 1998).

Danish universities are no exception to this. The recent reforms of Danish universities (especially the reform in 2007) were made with the policy intention to professionalize the university management but also to provide the universities with more organizational autonomy (Degn & Sørensen 2012, 2015). The governance model consisted of a new managerial structure with professional boards (with a majority of external members) that holds the leadership of the universities accountable, combined with development contracts, which specify performance goals for each university, between the Ministry of Higher Education and Science (henceforth abbreviated as "the ministry") and the board. This managerial model aligns with the steering-at-a-distance approach to university governance (Capano 2011) and should ensure local organizational autonomy at the universities. Organizational autonomy is defined as the universities' level of decision-making competencies (Enders et al. 2013: 11) and is primarily assigned to the professional management at the universities (the professional boards and the rector and deans).

However, public statements from different leaders at Danish universities and the evaluations of the University Act, on the contrary, suggest that this managerial structure has resulted in decreased autonomy and closer micromanagement (Ministry of Science 2009; Degn & Sørensen 2015). In this chapter we first take a closer look at the use of performance contracts at Danish universities and then search for possible explanations of why the use of performance contracts have resulted in less and not more autonomy. Thus, our research question is this:

> What might explain why steering-at-a-distance at Danish universities results in less not more autonomy?

We suggest two types of explanations for the reduced autonomy, each focusing on different levels in the specific government model at Danish universities.

First, we scrutinize the possibilities for autonomy in the general steering model. With departure in Capanos' typology of governance modes in higher education we look at the ministry's steering of the universities and explore how the board members and deans perceive the relationship between the ministry and the university. Our expectations are that the governance mode follows the principles from steering-from-a-distance and thereby provides the professional management at the universities with formal autonomy. The problem with decreased autonomy may also be linked to the organizational setup and the specific managerial model. The managerial model with boards and performance contracts corresponds nicely with a performance management approach, and should provide the universities with formal autonomy—at least in theory, but it may be quite different in practice. To investigate the level of real autonomy, we explore the board members' and deans' perception of how the managerial model works in practice and how this may affect the degrees of real autonomy. According to the board members the ministry is not using the managerial model correctly and engage in micromanagement and detailed regulation.

Second, to get a more comprehensive understanding of real autonomy, we explore the actual use of management tools (contracts and the performance measures within the contracts). We suggest that the lack of autonomy can be related to the way the performance contracts are designed and how university boards use the performance contracts in their steering process. Specifically, we look at the importance board members attach to the performance contracts and how the university boards use the performance contracts. We also look at how the deans see the use of performance contracts and its role in relation to the university strategy. We furthermore investigate the substantial content of the performance contracts, to see if they primarily consist of performance indicators (output and outcome measures) consistent with the steering-at-a-distance approach (Capano 2011: 1628) and thereby provide both formal and real autonomy (Enders et al. 2013; Christensen 2011). The analysis suggests that, even though the boards use the performance contracts according to the model, the content of the performance contracts can result in a feeling of reduced autonomy.

In this way, the chapter aims at a better understanding of the relationship between a PM-inspired governance model and both formal and real autonomy at Danish universities.

The chapter is structured as follows. In the next section we briefly introduce Capanos' typology of governance modes in higher education and discuss how this aligns with the theoretical performance management approach followed by a discussions about autonomy at universities. Hereafter we present how our data are used in this chapter. This section is followed by our analyses, where we focus on two possible explanations for reduced autonomy. Finally, we discuss our results and conclude the chapter.

Steering and Autonomy in Higher Education

The societal role of universities are also argued to be especially important in todays' knowledge-based economy (Degn & Sørensen 2015; Amaral & Magalhães 2004; Välimaa & Hoffman 2008), and this tendency causes a greater focus on performance at the universities (performance understood as research results and education of a skillful labor force [Bleiklie 1998]). Overall, the societal situation increases the need for political governance and strategic management of universities (Degn & Sørensen 2015: 932; Bleiklie & Byrkjeflot 2002). And "The basic features of past governance modes in higher education have been re-designed by recent governments, and in doing so they have also changed their role in the steering system" (Amaral, Jones & Karseth 2002; Huisman 2009; Paradeise, Reale, Bleiklie & Ferlie 2009 cited in Capano 2011: 1625). However, despite the many changes in the modern knowledge-based economy and the governance of the universities, a classical principal-agent relation still persists between the ministry (as principal) and the universities (as agents). A central issue in the literature on higher education governance therefore becomes how the principal can establish an incentive and control structure that makes the agent do what the principal wants (Enders et al. 2013). Therefore, Capano argues "in order to understand the intrinsic logic of governance shifts, we need to focus on the changing role of governments" (Capano 2011: 1625). And a central issue in this discussion is the question of the distribution of autonomy from the government to the universities. Thus, it is important to be aware of the ministry's role and the relationship between the ministry and the universities.

It is agreed, in the literature, that the recent reforms in higher education have caused a shift in the idea of autonomy. It is a shift from an emphasis on "professional autonomy" of academics inherent in the Humboldtian model, to an emphasis on a more market-oriented "organizational autonomy" given to a professional management at the universities in various New Public Management (NPM) models (Enders et al. 2013: 7–8; Christensen 2011). After the reforms, the autonomy is expected to be found in the relationships between the ministry and the professional management at the universities. In this chapter we will therefore focus our discussion on the managerial mechanisms in the relation between the ministry (the principal) and professional management at the universities. We will focus on the perception of autonomy in the professional boards, since they are expected to be the focal site where the new "organizational autonomy" should be most concentrated. With this focus, we limit the discussion of autonomy in universities to the relationship between formal autonomy and perceived autonomy however still acknowledging that other dimensions in the discussion of autonomy (for example cultural or environmental discussion [see for example Christensen 2011]) are important as well.

Steering-at-a-Distance at Danish Universities

To contribute to the understanding of changes in the governance of higher education, Capano has developed a typology of governance modes to describe and analyze the shifts in national governance modes within higher education (Capano 2011: 1623). This is based on two dimensions: (1) the level of government specification of the means to be used, and (2) the level of governmental specification of the goals to be achieved; four modes of governance are formed.

- procedural mode (high specification of means, low specification of goals),
- hierarchical mode (high specification of means, high specification of goals),
- steering-at-a-distance (low specification of means, high specification of goals), and
- self-governance mode (low specification of means, low specification of goals).

Capano points out that the role of the government (the principal) will vary according to the four different modes of governance. The "government may decide to model systemic governance through its choice of the degree of freedom to be afforded to other policy actors with regard to the goals to be pursued, and the means with which they are to be achieved"

(Capano 2011: 1626). Thus it is of analytical and empirical interest to clarify the role of the government and furthermore the relationships between the government and the agents in the specific managerial model if we want to get a better understanding of why and how autonomy is reduced by the new managerial model at the Danish universities.

Hierarchical governance and procedural governance represent traditional governance modes where Government uses direct control as the main steering tool. With regard to the question of autonomy it is the two latter governance modes; steering-at-a-distance, and the self-governance mode, which provide the universities with the highest degree of autonomy. In these two modes the Government influences the universities in a more indirect way using performance assessment and evaluations as the primary management approach (Capano 2011: 1627). The managerial model of the Danish universities can best be described as steering-at-a-distance. This governance mode rests upon the premise that the government states clearly defined performance goals, while leaving the universities with the autonomy to choose the means to reach the ends (the goals). In this way the reforms introduce a mode of governance that reflects a broader societal development towards New Public Management (NPM) and more specifically the use of Performance Management (PM) in the public sector (Degn & Sørensen 2015).

Autonomy and Performance Management at Universities

PM is a specific way for governments to steer-from-a-distance in higher education. PM is ideally designed to provide the agents with more autonomy at the local level. PM does so by holding the agent accountable for results and outcomes instead of steering through input and processes. The idea in PM is that the principal (the ministries) should set clear goals and define the results. Through continuous monitoring of the results, the principal can leave it to the agents (the universities) to define the means to reach those goals, and thereby provide the agents with more autonomy in the local managerial and financial decisions (Van Dooren, Bouckaert & Halligan 2010; Boyne 2010; Poister, Pasha & Edwards 2013). Thus PM involves a hierarchical structure that connect goal setting at the central principal level with the daily practical managerial decisions at the local agent level (Townley, Cooper & Oakes 2003). In this way PM is expected to provide the agents with a higher degree of local managerial and financial autonomy (what Enders et al. [2013] define as organizational autonomy), while reducing the autonomy in relation to goal setting and policy formulations.

The concept of autonomy is contested in the literature (Verhoest, Peters, Bouckaert & Verschuere 2004; Lægreid & Verhoest 2010).

Traditional universities have been granted a great deal of autonomy from the governments due to Academia's legitimacy in the protection of academic freedom. Under the Humboldtian model the universities were highly self-governed, the formal management was weak while the academics (the professors) were provided with autonomy and therefore they were the central actors in the managerial system at the universities (Enders et al. 2013: 7). However, the autonomy at universities has changed form and has been redistributed from the academics to a professional management after the reforms in the last 20–30 years. Results from the TRUE study show a great deal of variation in autonomy among European universities and variation between the different aspects of autonomy (Bleiklie et al. 2017)

The professional management at the universities (consisting of the professional boards, the rectors and the deans) has been empowered and is supposed to strengthen the universities as strategic organizational actors following the governments' policies and goals for higher education (Enders et al. 2013: 8). In this way a decentralization supported by performance management system, which provides a greater distance between the government and the universities, is taking place. In this sense steering at a distance is supposed to increase the formal autonomy located at the professional management. However, at the same time a recentralization of policy decisions and goals is also taking place and is likewise supported by the performance management systems and furthermore supported by the professionalization and empowerment of the university managements, thus decreasing the traditional form of academic or professional autonomy at the universities. Parallel to this, Christensen (2011) argue that the new NPM-inspired reforms formalize and intensify the steering dialog between ministries and universities, and by setting up professional boards and performance goals they redistribute the autonomy from the academic staff to the professional management. Enders et al. describe the changed ideas of autonomy in higher education in this way: "A new narrative about university autonomy has thus been emerging in which the university as an organization has become an important focus of attention in the system's coordination" (Enders et al. 2013: 9). This means that the reforms have caused a redistribution in autonomy at the universities where the formal organizational autonomy has been strengthened, while the cultural and academic autonomy has been weakened (see also Christensen 2011: 512).

Thus, from these discussion of university reforms (Degn & Sørensen 2015; Enders et al. 2013; Christensen 2011), it should be expected that the formal organizational autonomy is increased and located within the professional management after the university reforms, while other dimensions of autonomy especially the professional autonomy is decreased at the universities. However, studies have discussed if and how PM provides the local management with more formal organizational autonomy (Van Dooren, Voets & Winters 2015; Verschuere 2007; Moynihan 2008, 2006). Moynihan for example shows that there is a great focus on establishing monitoring systems when PM is introduced in public organizations, the aspects of increased autonomy is often neglected (Moynihan 2008, 2006). Moreover, Christensen argues that it is important to differ between formal autonomy and real autonomy at universities. In a comparison between the "traditional university systems" and the new systems after the reforms, he proposes that the recent university reforms with its PM-inspired modes of governance in general increase the formal distance between ministries and universities (Christensen 2011: 509) and thereby provide the universities with more formal autonomy. But at the same time the reforms decrease the real autonomy by introducing standardized rules for different activities and performance management systems with inherent incentive systems as well as scrutiny and control of goals. This makes the discussion of autonomy more complicated since "there is definitely a dynamic and potentially tension-filled relationship between control and autonomy, making it rather difficult to judge the actual autonomy of universities following modern reforms" (Christensen 2011: 510). Furthermore, Enders et al. write that

> changes in the formal autonomy situation of universities do matter but there are good reasons to assume that autonomy in practice is not a perfect copy of formal autonomy. Formal rules for autonomy might be implemented or not, and they cannot prescribe in advance practices in universities.
>
> (Enders et al. 2013, pp. 10)

Research has focused on the implementation of PM and steering-at-a-distance within higher education. There are also studies of autonomy in higher education (for example Bleiklie et al. 2017; Christensen 2011; Enders et al. 2013; Degn & Søernsen 2015; Ordorika 2003), however the major part of these studies discuss the theoretical conceptualization of autonomy in higher education. Therefore we still lack knowledge of how reforms (as we have seen in higher education in Denmark and other Western countries) affect the real autonomy located at the university management in practice. We know very little of these tension-filled relationships of control and actual autonomy at universities in practice, and almost nothing about the governance relationships and the actual distribution of autonomy between the ministries and the professional management and university boards. Therefore we will explore the relationships between the ministry and the professional boards at the university to get a more comprehensive understanding of the distribution of formal and real autonomy in higher education in Denmark. We focus on the relationship between the ministry and the professional management by exploring the board members and the deans' perceptions of the universities' level of decision-making competencies (their perception of organizational autonomy).

First, we ask if the governance mode is designed as a steering-from-a-distance model that provides the professional management at the universities with formal autonomy as expected. We scrutinize the organizational setup and the specific managerial model at Danish universities to get a better understanding of if and how the formal autonomy provided by the specific managerial model is translated into real autonomy in practice. Finally we go deeper into the discussion of real autonomy at the universities by looking at how the board members use the performance contracts in their managerial decision processes and what measures are actually characterizing the contracts thereby defining the real level of decision-making competencies.

Data and Measurements

The Danish university sector is an interesting case when investigating why performance management leads to less autonomy—and not more autonomy as expected. Traditionally universities have been agents with a high degree of autonomy. Furthermore the recent reforms of Danish universities were made with the policy intention to professionalize the university management but also to provide the universities with more autonomy (Degn & Sørensen 2012).

In this chapter, we use data from a survey with all members of the Danish university boards carried out in 2014. In the survey with board members we had a number of questions trying to tap into the four modes of governance suggested by Capano—see Table 7.1. We tried to group the questions into the four models using factor analysis. However, it was not possible to fit the answers in the four groups. We are not aware of any well-tested set of questions to capture the four modes of governance and the questions used may not have been the right ones. In the following, we will therefore just refer to the frequencies. Second, we include interviews with chairs of the boards, statutes, minutes from board meetings, and self-evaluations. The quotes used in this chapter were translated from Danish to English by the authors. Third, we have interviewed eight deans representing different universities and different academic fields. Fourth, we collected all development contracts between the ministry and each university from 2005 to 2015. The contracts were coded according to number of measures and type of measure. We coded for four different types of measures: input, process, output, and outcome measures. If it was estimated that there were several measures in one measure, it was coded as two different measures. The measures can be perceived from different perspectives (e.g., the ministry, the students or the university). In the coding, each measure was perceived from the perspective of the universities. When it was estimated whether a measure was an input or output measure it was decided based on the university's point of view.[1] Chapter 2 in this book gives for a more thorough description of the data used in the analysis.

Table 7.1 How do board members perceive the ministry's steering of the universities?

	Agree/fully agree
Procedural mode	
Detailed national regulations exist for the procedure in connection with recruiting employees for the university	29%
The ministry makes demands on the organization of the internal management of the university	26%
The ministry manages through approval procedures	52%
Hierarchical mode	
The ministry manages through earmarked funds	60%
The ministry regulates the content of the study programs	31%
The ministry determines goals for the research results	23%
Steering at a distance	
The ministry manages research and education through financial incentives	87%
The ministry manages through contracts	85%
The ministry manages through the use of assessments	53%
Self-governance mode	
The ministry reserves the right to intervene, but leaves the management to each individual institution	61%
The ministry regulates through negotiations and persuasion	26%
The ministry leaves the coordination of the sector to the universities	24%

Analyses

The policy intention behind the recent reforms of Danish universities was to professionalize the university management and to provide the universities with more autonomy (Degn & Sørensen 2012). The governance model consisted of a new managerial model with professional boards (with a majority of external member) combined with performance contracts between the ministry and the board. This structure aligns with the steering-at-a-distance approach to university governance (Capano 2011) and should ensure autonomy at the universities. However, it is questionable whether the introduction of this managerial model resulted in more autonomy, and the formal evaluation of the University Act (Ministry of Science 2009) pointed to problems with more control and micromanagement by the ministry. In the following, we will look for possible explanations for this. We suggest two types of explanations, and each focuses on different levels of the managerial model:

1. the ministry's steering of the universities and the managerial model, and
2. the importance and use of contracts in the managerial model.

First, we will try to categorize the modes of steering from the ministry using the board members' perceptions of which managerial tools the ministry actually applies in practice. This analysis will provide an empirical evaluation of how aligned the overall governance system is with the steering-at-a-distance mode, described by Capano. We will also go deeper into the specific managerial model at Danish universities and investigate if the steering process follows the principles of "distance" or "arm's length" between the ministry and the universities which are embedded in the model. This analysis will give us knowledge about if and how the ministry steers at a distance. Second, we will take a closer look at a specific part of the managerial model, namely the contracts. We will explore how important the board members and the deans find the contracts and how they use them in their managerial decisions. This will help us asses how much impact the performance contracts actually have on the boards' managerial decisions. The argument is that the measures in the performance contracts also determine if the overall model provides the universities with more or less autonomy. If the measures in the contract primarily consist of output and outcome measures, then it follows the classical PM literature and increased autonomy should be expected, while decreased autonomy should be expected if the measures primarily consist of process and input measures.

The Ministry's Steering of the Universities and the Management Model

The state can control and steer the universities in different ways. Capano (2011) differs between procedural mode, hierarchical mode, steering-at-a-distance, and self-governance mode to describe how the state can manage the universities We have asked how the board members perceive the ministry's use of different policy instruments related to each of the four governance modes are presented in Table 7.1.

One the one hand, in board members' experience, the ministry uses policy instruments associated with performance management/steering at a distance such as contracts, economic incentives, and assessments. It is the mode of governance that stands out the most. On the other hand, the ministry also uses other policy instruments related to other modes of steering. The board members find that the ministry uses earmarked funds and regulates through approval procedures as well. According to the board members, it is a mix of different modes of governance and specific instruments that is used in relation to universities. The combination of steering-at-a-distance/performance management and a number of other policy instruments shows a very mixed and comprehensive steering mode.

The picture presented by the survey data is supported by the chairmen. During the interviews the chairmen were critical towards the ministry's steering. Some of the critical comments target specific elements of the ministry's steering and will be elaborated in the following sections, but there were also some more general comments on the steering. In general, the chairmen found that the steering is too detailed. As one chairman puts it:

> The ministry use[s] the gas pedal, hits the brakes, turns the wheel and use[s] the gear-shift all at once. The one hand removes rules while the other hand introduces new rules.

When talking to the deans, they describe a similar mix of steering and management instruments. They all see the performance contracts and performance management as one characteristic of the steering paradigm, but they also see many other ways that the ministry tries to control the universities. One dean mentioned that the steering is a combination of a performance orientation and an obsession with control and lack of trust. Another says:

> It is the economic regulation through the state budget that has the largest effect and then the detailed regulation—the ministry's inter-pretation, reinterpretation and new interpretation of the rules we have to observe.

Several mention a specific and very detailed regulation of the number of credits students must pass every semester as an example of the type of regulation that comes in addition to performance contracts.

The organizational model with boards as the link between the ministry (the owner) and the rector (management of the university) are well suited for an arm's length approach and implementation of a performance man-agement system. The ministry enters into a contract with the board that then must account for the performance of the university and the fulfil-ment of the contract (and control the management of the university). The model gives the ministry the possibility to be at arm's length of the university. However, according to the chairmen of the university boards this is not how the model works. On the contrary—and as mentioned previously—they experience very detailed regulation and interference in day-to-day processes. One chairman mentioned:

> The most comic example was an order to measure all the bookshelves at the university.

The deans also experience a ministry that engages in micromanagement and uses very detailed regulations. Some even argue that there has been a change from a framework management approach to a much more detail-oriented approach. When asked about whether there is an arm's length principle between the ministry and the university, a dean has the following comment:

> Yes, but the arm has become shorter and shorter and the ministry has somewhat of a bailiff mentality.

Several of the chairmen argue that the ministry—or part of the ministry—doesn't understand the organizational model with boards and how it is supposed to work. One chairman describes it in the following way:

> They by-pass the board and make detailed regulation. It is a thorn in the side of not only me but also of the board. They don't give the universities free. They just seek influence through other channels than the board.

According to the board governance model the ministry should act through the board and use the performance contract as the main vehicle for controlling and steering the board. The problem according to one chairman is that the bureaucrats in the ministry don't know how to run a proper governance system. Another chairman mentions that the problem is not the minister or the top bureaucrats, but the agency in charge of the universities. The argument was that the former had understood the governance system and had a genuine interest in giving the universities more autonomy, while the latter is afraid of losing control and acts as if the organizational setup hasn't changed. The agency will lose some of its controlling power if the performance contract becomes the main steering document. Thus the interviews hinted that even though there had been major reforms in higher education latest in 2007, the governments' role was still not clear. Capano argues that the governments' role may shift in the different governance modes (Capano 2011: 1625). Maybe the government had not been entirely aware of the changes the steering-at-a-distance model would have for its own role in the governance, but primarily focused on changes at the universities with the reforms. Or maybe there still was a political (but more hidden) wish for a closer micromanagement. The explanation might also lie in the different political roles and tasks the minister and the agency respectively take care of. The minister may state the overall goals, while the agency is in higher need of a closer control and therefore introduces more detailed regulations parallel to the ministry goals. The different observations from the chairmen and deans don't give a full account of how the organizational setup works. It would be relevant to get the opinion of the ministry and how they experience the system. Nevertheless, the statements from the chairmen and the deans give a strong indication that part of the problem with the reduced autonomy may be related to how the management system is run and a lack of understanding of the organizational setup—especially the role of the government in that setup.

The Performance Contracts

The performance contract is an agreement between the ministry and the university boards and it is signed by the chairman of the board. The contract contains a number of performance targets that the university must fulfil and must account for by the end of the contract period. There have been different frameworks for the content of the performance contract, but for the most part it has included common performance targets for all universities determined by the ministry, supplemented by a target defined by the individual university. In the following, we first look at how the boards use the contract and how it affects strategies and plans at the university. Second, we investigate the content of the contracts and see if they support more autonomy to the universities.

Use of Contracts

The performance contract between the ministry and the university is an important element in the performance management system. It is supposed to be the key document where the state's expectation of the performance of the university is stated. In return for fulfilling the objectives stated in the performance contract the university should be given more autonomy. In a steering-from-a-distance approach it should be expected that the boards emphasize the contract in their work and use it as an important element in developing the strategy of the university. In the survey with members of the university boards, we have asked about the role of performance contracts and how they use the performance contracts—see Table 7.2.

Table 7.2 How do university boards use performance contracts?

Use of performance contracts	Agree/fully agree
There is a close connection between the strategy and the development contract with the ministry	64%
The consideration for fulfilling the development contract is vital for the board's decisions	54%
It forms the basis for prioritizing resources	52%
The development contract is often discussed at board meetings	42%
It is the overall management tool for the board's management of the university	30%

The performance contracts play an important role in connection to the strategy of the universities. Almost two-thirds of the board members agrees or fully agrees that there is a close connection between the contract and the strategy of the university. In other words, the objectives from the performance contract seem to find its way into the organization through the strategy process. Furthermore, about half of the board members find the fulfillment of the performance contract to be vital for the board's decisions or the basis for prioritizing resources.

The deans view to some extent the development contract and its relation to the strategy the same way as expressed by the board members, but are at the same time more critical. One the one hand, it is evident that the deans take the development contracts serious both as members of the top management team of the university and in relation to their own faculty/school. They are also concerned with the fulfilment of the performance targets and pay attention how they perform. Several of the deans describe a procedure where they regularly score how they are doing on the specific performance targets. Some mention that the performance contracts help to specify what the political level wants and what their intentions are for the development of the universities. On the other hand, it is also evident that the development contracts are not a key instrument for the management or the development of the universities. Most of the deans point to the many changes that occur with the performance targets and objectives that are included in the development contract. They describe how changing ministers have added new objectives and targets to the contracts, which makes it difficult to use in relation to the management of the university. When it comes to the relationship between the development contract and the strategy of the university, it is a common view among the deans that the general objectives put into the contract by the ministry overlap with interests of the university. One example mentioned by a dean is the internationalization of research and education where there are common interests. The deans are more critical towards how the objectives are measured and how to establish a baseline. Based on the statements from the deans, it is also obvious that they consider the university strategy far more important than the development contract. Whereas the strategy is an important document for the development of the university, the development contract is something that need to be handled and for some "a necessary evil".

Contents in the Contracts

There seems to be a relationship between the development contract and the strategy of the university even though the boards report a closer relationship than the deans do. In that light, it is relevant to take a closer look at the content of the contracts.

We looked at performance contracts between the ministry and each university from 2005 to 2015. The study shows that the total number of measuring point in the contracts have decreased from 422 in 2006 to 210 in 2015. This should be expected in a steering-from-a-distance model based on performance management, since performance management builds on a few but clearly stated goals (Hood 1991). It is furthermore expected that there was a development over time and changes initiated by the reforms could be traced. We would, for example, expect a shift towards more output and outcome goals and less input and process goals after 2007. However, when looking at the different types of measures, we see some fluctuation—see Figure 7.1. In the contracts covering the period, process and input measures were dominant. In the following years process measures decreased while output measures increased as expected. We also do see a reduction in the number of process measures in the middle of the period, but from 2012 this type of measurement point increased again towards the end of the period. This hints that something happened after 2011, but officially no alterations were made to the governance model. The number of outcome measures has remained low during the entire period compared to other types of measures. This is contrary to the recommendations in performance management that particularly emphasize a steering through an increased focus on outcome measures (Van Dooren et al. 2010). Hence, this is also a surprising result. In 2015 input and process measures accounted for more than 70 percent of the total number of measurement point in the contracts. We have argued that input and process measures tend to give the universities less autonomy than output and outcome measures. Based on this premise Danish universities have not experienced increased formal autonomy due to the use of performance management. In fact, based on the development the past

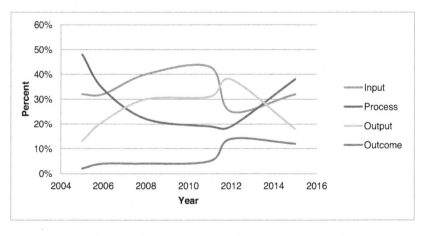

Figure 7.1 Distribution of types of measures from 2005–2015

couple of years, it looks like the universities experience a decrease in formal autonomy.

As shown earlier, the performance contracts have a majority of input and process measures. When the boards are faced with this type of measures and at the same time use the performance contract as basis for strategy and prioritization of resources, it can result in a feeling of reduced autonomy and may generate frustration among the board members and deans. This development supports our points in the previous analyses that other management tools are at stake in the Danish governance model for higher education.

Discussion and Conclusion

We asked why steering-at-a-distance at Danish universities results in less and not more autonomy. We presented two types of explanations that to some degree are interrelated. First, we looked at the overall steering mode using the typology by Capano. In the Danish case, it is obvious that it is not only steering-at-a-distance that is used. On the contrary, there is a mix of steering modes and policy instruments used to control and influence the universities that result in a very detailed type of regulation. Based on statements from the chairmen of the boards and deans we find evidence that the ministry (or maybe just the agency) does not entirely understand how to use a governance model with boards as the intermediary between the ministry and the management of the universities. Second, we show that the performance contracts are used as the basis for decisions by the board, but because the content of the contracts is dominated by input and process measures it may result in a feeling of reduced rather than increased autonomy.

The analysis of the governance model used by the ministry in relation to the Danish universities is in line with Moynihan's argument that the reforms have had a greater focus on establishing goals and evaluating systems than providing the local agents with more autonomy (Moynihan 2009). Van Dooren and colleagues furthermore discuss how performance management simply adds another layer of control to the existing regulations and thereby decreases rather than increases the local autonomy. They argue that the intention of giving the agents increased autonomy through decentralization of decision-making can generate control mechanisms to a degree, which might undermine the autonomy initially given. Instead of a simplified control system, control is layered in a process of reregulation (Van Dooren et al. 2015). These reregulating mechanisms also seem to be at stake in the Danish governance of higher education. We saw in the analysis of the content of the performance contracts, that a remarkably shift was taking place in the years 2011 and 2012. However, no official alterations were announced in relation to the reforms, and the policy intentions in higher education in Denmark still remained the same.

This indicates that the governance mode was exposed to a more indirect form of reregulation through layering. We cannot determine whether this reregulation was a deliberate choice on the minster's part, or just a consequence of old practices and need for control in the agency were slowly reintroduced. However, it blurs the picture and results in an unclear, mixed governance model, where the agents (the universities) experience a loss of autonomy.

However, not all parts of the governance model are unclear and mixed. The performance contracts were adopted by the boards, which used them to guide their work. But exactly this point of the system might as well explain why the universities experience the reforms as a reduction of their autonomy. When the content of the contracts focus more on input and process measures as discussed earlier, the contract may be contrary to the intentions of performance management and contribute to increased micromanagement. Soss, Fording, and Schramm (2011) explain how PM introduces new incentives in work and thereby discipline the daily practice of the public managers and employees in an indirect but more regulated way (Soss et al. 2011, see also Dias & Maynard-Moody 2007). The performance contracts used by the boards may have the same function. They state clear goals with linked incentives and when the boards are guided by them, as reported in our survey, they may have a significant impact on the lower levels of management at the universities.

Capano concludes that government continues to govern and has not lost any of its policy-making power, but it has simply changed the way it steers higher education (Capano 2011: 1622). There is no doubt in our case that the government continues to govern. However, the shift towards steering-at-a-distance is much more unclear, even though the reforms were designed to steer-at-a-distance ideally. We have pointed at specific mechanisms through which the government use a steering-at-a-distance approach but at the same time use very close micromanagement. Part of the literature on governance in higher education discusses how the reforms have resulted in a movement away from the Humboldt university tradition and placed the power and influence in the hands of the management. Our analysis suggests that the situation is much more complex and that the modes of governance in higher education are contradictory.

The chapter contributes to the existing research in several ways. First, the analyses focus on formal organizational autonomy at Danish universities after the recent reforms. This perspective goes beyond traditional approaches focusing on the legal status of the public organizations (Enders et al. 2013: 13). Furthermore, the chapter goes beyond the existing discussions in the literature of a shift from the Humboldtian tradition to NPM-inspired managerial modes by placing a specific focus on the formal organizational autonomy at universities today. Second, the chapter contributes with a discussion of both formal and real organizational autonomy. In general a better understanding of the real autonomy at universities are highly needed in the research (Enders et al. 2013: 13), and until now no studies (that we are aware of) have investigated if the managements are actually provided with real organizational autonomy as expected in recent research. We contribute with a thorough understanding of the level of real autonomy at Danish universities after the reforms by scrutinizing several aspects of the actual managerial practice with performance contracts and follow the development of the contracts over time. Third, based on our analyses, we argue that despite a higher level of formal organizational autonomy in the managerial model, the real organizational autonomy is still limited because of several parallel managerial regulations between the ministry and the universities. These empirical insights question some of the central assumptions in the discussion of autonomy and management at universities today. The chapter offers a counterpoint to the dominant assumption: the autonomy should be moved from the academics to professional management. Our analyses show that there is only a limited real autonomy at the professional management level, and we discuss the nature of the shifts in autonomy that is actually taking place and try to give an explanation of why this misfit between formal and real autonomy occur. In this way, we try to inspire a more nuanced understanding of the shifts in autonomy after the reforms.

Note

1. An example of where there is a difference depending on perspective is external funds. To the Ministry, a goal of increasing external funds can be perceived as an output measure. To each university, external funds are something that changes input, in the sense that it adds resources in order to achieve certain outputs. Based on the same logic, establishing new education programs can be perceived as an output for the Ministry, but an input for each university.

References

Amaral, A., Jones, G. & Karseth, B. 2002, *Governing Higher Education: National Perspectives on Institutional Governance*, Kluwer Academic Publishers, Dordrecht.

Amaral, A. & Magalhães, A. 2004, "Epidemiology and the Bologna Saga", *Higher Education (00181560)*, vol. 48, no. 1, pp. 79–100.

Bleiklie, I. 1998, "Justifying the Evaluative State: New Public Management Ideals in Higher Education", *European Journal of Education*, vol. 33, no. 3, pp. 299–316.

Bleiklie, I. & Kogan, M. 2007, "Organization and Governance of Universities", *Higher Education Policy*, vol. 20, no. 4, pp. 477–493.

Bleiklie, I. & Byrkjeflot, H. 2002, "Changing Knowledge Regimes: Universities in a New Research Environment", *Higher Education*, vol. 44, no. 3–4, pp. 519–532.

Bleiklie, I., Enders, J. & Lepori, B. 2017, *Managing Universities: Policy and Organizational Change From a Western European Comparative Perspective*, Springer International Publishing, Cham, Switzerland.

Boyne, G.A. 2010, "Performance Management: Does It Work?", in *Public Management and Performance: Research Directions*, eds. R.M. Walker, G.A. Boyne & G.A. Brewer, Cambridge University Press, Cambridge, pp. 207–226.

Capano, G. 2011, "Government Continues to Do Its Job. A Comparative Study of Governance Shifts in the Higher Education Sector", *Public Administration*, vol. 89, no. 4, pp. 1622–1642.

Christensen, T. 2010, "University Governance Reform—Putting Japanese Experience Into Perspective", *The Journal of Finance and Management in Colleges and Universities*, vol. 7, pp. 205–229.

Christensen, T. 2011, "University Governance Reforms: Potential Problems of More Autonomy?", *Higher Education*, vol. 62, no. 4, pp. 503–517.

Christensen, T. & Lægreid, P. 2007, *Transcending New Public Management*, Ashgate, Surrey.

Degn, L. & Sørensen, M.P. 2012, "Universitetsloven fra 2003. På vej mod konkurrenceuniversitetet?", in *Dansk forskningspolitik efter årtusindeskiftet*, eds. K. Aagaard & N. Mejlgaard, Aarhus Universitetsforlag, Aarhus.

Degn, L. & Sørensen, M.P. 2015, "From Collegial Governance to Conduct of Conduct: Danish Universities Set Free in the Service of the State", *Higher Education*, vol. 69, no. 6, pp. 931; 946–946.

Dias, J.J. & Maynard-Moody, S. 2007, "For-Profit Welfare: Contracts, Conflicts, and the Performance Paradox", *Journal of Public Administration Research and Theory*, vol. 17, no. 2, pp. 189–211.

Enders, J., de Boer, H. & Weyer, E. 2013, "Regulatory Autonomy and Performance: The Reform of Higher Education Re-visited", *Higher Education*, vol. 65, no. 1, pp. 5–23.

Hood, C. 1991, "A Public Management for All Seasons?", *Public Administration*, vol. 69, no. 1, pp. 3–19.

Huisman, J. 2009, *International Perspectives on the Governance of Higher Education*, Routledge, London.

Kettl, D. 2000, *The Global Public Management Revolution*, Brookings Institution Press, Washington, DC.

Lægreid, P. & Verhoest, K. 2010, *Governance of Public Sector Organizations: Proliferation, Autonomy and Performance*, Palgrave Macmillan, London.

Ministry of Science, Technology and Innovation. 2009, *The University Evaluation 2009*, Copenhagen.

Moynihan, D.P. 2006, "Managing for Results in State Government: Evaluating a Decade of Reform", *Public Administration Review*, vol. 66, no. 1, pp. 77–89.

Moynihan, D.P. 2008, *The Dynamics of Performance Management: Constructing Information and Reform*, Georgetown University Press, Washington, DC.

Moynihan, D.P. 2009, "Through a Glass, Darkly", *Public Performance & Management Review*, vol. 32, no. 4, pp. 592–603.

Ordorika, I. 2003, "The Limits of University Autonomy: Power and Politics at the Universidad Nacional Autónoma de México", *Higher Education*, vol. 46, no. 3, pp. 361–388.

Paradeise, C., Reale, E., Bleiklie, I. & Ferlie, E. 2009, *University Governance: Western European Comparative Perspectives*, Springer, Dordrecht.

Poister, T.H., Pasha, O.Q. & Edwards, L.H. 2013, "Does Performance Management Lead to Better Outcomes? Evidence From the U.S. Public Transit Industry", *Public Administration Review*, vol. 73, no. 4, pp. 625–636.

Pollitt, C. & Bouckaert, G. 2017, *Public Management Reform: A Comparative Analysis—Into the Age of Austerity*, Fourth edn, Oxford University Press, Oxford.

Rainey, H.G. 2009, *Understanding and Managing Public Organizations*, Jossey-Bass, San Francisco.

Soss, J., Fording, R. & Schram, S.F. 2011, "The Organization of Discipline: From Performance Management to Perversity and Punishment", *Journal of Public Administration Research and Theory: J-PART*, vol. 21, no. Supplement 2, pp. i203–i232.

Townley, B., Cooper, D.J. & Oakes, L. 2003, "Performance Measures and the Rationalization of Organizations", *Organization Studies*, vol. 24, no. 7, pp. 1045–1071.

Välimaa, J. & Hoffman, D. 2008, "Knowledge Society Discourse and Higher Education", *Higher Education*, vol. 56, no. 3, pp. 265–285.

Van Dooren, W., Bouckaert, G. & Halligan, J. 2010, *Performance Management in the Public Sector*, Routledge, London.

Van Dooren, W., Voets, J. & Winters, S. 2015, "Autonomy and Regulation: Explaining Dynamics in the Flemish Social Housing Sector", *Public Administration*, vol. 93, no. 4, pp. 1068–1083.

Verhoest, K., Peters, B.G., Bouckaert, G. & Verschuere, B. 2004, "The Study of Organisational Autonomy: A Conceptual Review", *Public Administration and Development*, vol. 24, no. 2, pp. 101–118.

Verschuere, B. 2007, "The Autonomy—Control Balance in Flemish Arm's Length Public Agencies", *Public Management Review*, vol. 9, no. 1, pp. 107–133.

8 Academics and Performance Systems

Poul Erik Mouritzen and Niels Opstrup

Introduction

Using different types of incentives schemes to guide and to improve performance are an integral part of the mindset of New Public Management (NPM) (Barzelay 2001; Swiss 2005). Incentives schemes are applied towards as well the organizational level as sub-organizational levels or individual employees within public organizations. This is also the case at Danish universities: a so-called performance-based research funding system (Hicks 2012), the Bibliometric Research Indicator (BRI), is used to allocate part of the universities' base funding according to the quantity and quality of research output (Mouritzen & Opstrup 2019). Within the universities, different systems that monitor the performance of subunits and allocate resources based on their results have been set up in many places; it has also become more and more common to implement incentive systems which reward or punish the individual researcher according to his or her research performance. The latter takes the form of either performance-related pay schemes (Andersen & Pallesen 2008), access to departmental resources, or "publication command systems", which specify the minimum number of journal articles required from each researcher combined with principles for how this is monitored and sanctioned (Jacobsen & Andersen 2014: 85). One type of sanction used at some departments is increased teaching loads.

At the extreme one can imagine a series of principal-agent relations linking central government research agencies with the individual university scholar, relations where the principal monitors the performance of the agent and rewards or imposes costs accordingly. Central in the principal-agent theory are *agency problems* that occur if the agents' preferences differ from those of the principal and therefore give them reason to misrepresent the principal's interests. Such agency problems are an unavoidable risk in modern organizations due to the information asymmetries and moral hazards inherent in the specialization and division of labor. However, principals can mitigate these potential agency problems by introducing outcome-based incentives that align the incentives agents face with the preferences of the principal (Miller 2005), e.g., by linking pay to fulfillment of (organizational) performance goals. Reinforcement theory (Skinner 1953) notes that individuals will respond to stimuli and adjust their behavior depending on the consequences (retrospectively) (Stajkovic & Luthans 1997). Expectancy theory (Vroom 1964) correspondingly states that individuals' motivation to exert an effort will depend on their (prospective) perceived probability of whether a particular performance level leads to a given level of reward (Steel & König 2006). In short, incentives will raise *extrinsic motivation*.

Critique of result-based incentives is abundant. According to one line of thinking, public employees should work "not just for the money" (Frey 1997). Rewards sometimes produce hidden costs (Lepper & Greene 1978). A use of (extrinsic) incentives can diminish or even destroy intrinsic motivation through a so-called *crowding-out effect* (Frey 1997; Frey & Oberholzer-Gee 1997; Frey & Jegen 2001; Weibel, Rost & Osterloh 2010).

In the same vein, opponents of performance-based measures and incentives discuss a number of unintended consequences or behavioral reactions of public employees in general (e.g., de Bruijn 2007; Radin 2006; Bevan & Hood 2006; van Thiel & Leeuw 2002; Smith 1995) and researchers in particular (see Osterloh 2010: 274–276). Employees are expected to act strategically in order to "game the system". They will meet the target but at the expense of quality; goal displacement may take place; and slicing, creaming, and even cheating may become more prevalent. Within academia it is said to give rise to "slicing strategies" where researchers increase their publication counts by dividing their articles to a least publishable unit (Weingart 2005), the "prostitution of ideas" in order to getting published (Frey 2003), and cause a homogenization of knowledge production that discourages creative, unorthodox, and idiosyncratic research (Gillies 2008)

Proponents and skeptics, however, share one common assumption: if management decides to implement control or reward regime, the employees will know the rules of the game and act accordingly. Systems are implemented flawlessly. Proponents assume that the selfish agent knows the rules and, if the system is set up in a clever way, he or she will do everything to meet the preferences of the principal. The skeptics similarly assume that the selfish agent knows the rules and will do everything he or she can to circumvent them while at the same time meeting the target. This common assumption may be totally wrong. What if incentive systems are not implemented flawlessly? Could it be that management has an interest in keeping the rules unclear, ambiguous, and arbitrary? Or could it be that employees have different incentives and/or opportunities to seek or get information about the incentive system? What if you know about the system only if you by coincidence happened to be at a particular place at a particular time?

The chapter assumes that a relatively large part of the target population is in fact unaware of the existence of incentive systems at their department. The aim is to understand why ignorance of control and of reward systems is a widespread phenomenon among highly educated people working at institutions of higher education. It is generally expected that ignorance will be more widespread the less people have a chance to obtain rewards or be hit by sanctions. Also, it is expected that leadership attention to individual scholars' performance as well as leadership attention to the enforcement of the system will be important for the perception of individuals.

The analysis is based on the survey of faculty members at 66 Danish university departments.

Incentive Systems at Danish Universities

A performance-based system rewarding good (or plenty!) research or punishing underperformers ideally assumes a recurring cycle: In the first step, a set of rules is established, defining the criteria upon which faculty members are rewarded or punished (fixed targets may be part of the rules, but are rarely found in the research sector), the conditions that will result in either a reward or a penalty, and finally the exact nature (size/strength) of the reward or penalty. In the second step, the performance of the researcher is appraised, either through a system of continuous monitoring or periodically—typically once a year. In the third step, the department chair will follow up and evaluate performance against the established criteria. Finally, in the last step, the individual researcher will receive the reward or the penalty. As we shall see in the following sections, things are often quite different in the real world.

First of all, in the Danish setting labor unions have on paper a strong say when it comes to performance-related pay. At some departments the local representative will be heavily involved in the formulation of the rules, at others he or she will play almost no role. More importantly, the local union representative will participate on an equal basis with management (typically the dean and/or the department chair) when the annual decisions on bonuses are made.[1] This system is, however, not valid for full professors who are entitled to deal directly with management. Second, yearly bonuses as well as permanent pay increases are often not given automatically according to explicit criteria. The individual faculty member has to apply for increases and set up supportive arguments often based unclear and ambiguous criteria or, as the second alternative, the department chair may nominate employees for a one-time bonus or permanent salary increase with reference to particular meritorious activities during the previous period. Finally, at some departments, bonuses in particular may not be based on research performance but performance in other areas like excellent teaching, the development of study programs, administrative functions, or performance in the media, the underlying logic being that excellent researchers are rewarded via the normal career system. Departments differ a lot with respect to the criteria used. Among the university departments studied, bonuses are given often or exclusively for research in 21 cases. In another 21 departments bonuses are never or only rarely given for research. In the remaining 21 bonuses are given sometimes for research.[2]

Second, management will sometimes exhibit a preference for broad, diffuse, and ambiguous rules and procedures for at least three reasons. Department chairs often prefer discretionary to clear and binding rules in order to be able to act "according to the situation" at hand. Contingencies may arise that require action, and even detailed rules are rarely exhaustive. In the minutes from a meeting between dean and department chairs it was stated that "there was general satisfaction among the department chairs that the rules about permanent salary increases were flexible". A second reason why managers may prefer diffuse to precise rules is related to the economic situation of the department and faculty. Departments which have experienced drastic reductions in their student enrollment obviously have few means for bonuses and permanent increases, others are in the opposite situation. The former situation is not one that invites for large, automatic rule-bound salary regulations. A third major reason for diffuse performance regimes is related to the target group. Until a couple of decades ago salaries at Danish universities were fixed by national collective agreements. The number of professorships in the different grades were similarly fixed in the national budget. Today deans and department chairs can actively design compensation packages in order to retain attractive faculty members or recruit top level or promising scholars from other universities (Andersen, Eriksson, Kristensen & Pedersen 2012). The need to be able to act quickly in such a situation presupposes discretionary rules. Finally, one cannot exclude the possibility that unclear rules may actually make employees work harder. Clear, automatic, and attractive bonuses related to research will make people perform in the research area maybe at the expense of other important tasks. However, if employees know about the existence of a pay for performance system but they do not know the details of that system, they may try to perform well on all relevant dimensions.

As indicated previously, departments differ quite a lot with respect to the importance of research performance for one-time bonuses or permanent salary increases. When it comes to the exact rules they differ even more. Here we present three different systems found among Danish university departments.[3]

Department A. Despite options to add to the dean's rules, make them more precise, or even introduce an element of automatic pay increases, this department relies solely on the system established by the dean. According to this, one-time bonuses may (not "will") be given in case a faculty member has accomplished a special effort in the areas of research, external funding, dissemination of research, community service as well as development of new study programs and high-quality teaching. The remuneration scale consists of two levels. The normal level is €2400 while an extraordinary effort may result in €4800.[4] The latter amount comes close the monthly salary of an assistant professor.

Department B. One-time bonuses are given to faculty members who obtain external resources for research as well as teaching exceeding €67,000. The bonus is 2 percent of the amount obtained. Articles in a level 2 journal (according to the list established by the Danish Ministry of Science, Innovation and Higher Education) is rewarded with €800. Articles published in a journal of extraordinary repute (list established by the Department) is rewarded with €1300. A research monograph published at an internal publisher of repute (based on list established by the ministry) is rewarded with €1600.[5]

Department C. Faculty members who attract external research funds are awarded with 7 percent of the total sum (the departments' share of overhead costs). Five percent is given as a sum to be used via the department according to the rules of the university while 2 percent is given as a one-time bonus (personal income). Active researchers who perform above a certain level may have their teaching load reduced by 50 percent. Faculty members who underperform may have their teaching load increased by 1/3 or more. Faculty members who are active in the media may obtain a yearly one-time bonus of up to €5300.[6]

These schemes are rather different. Since the (diffuse) criteria cover all aspects of a faculty member's daily activities, the dean at Department A is able to reward efforts at his own discretion with rather few strings attached. For the individual employee who strives for a salary increase the result of any effort is quite uncertain. At Department B, all one-time bonuses are released automatically once the criteria have been fulfilled. No discretion is left to management and the individual employee knows with certainty whether a given result will lead to a reward. At Department C "reward certainty" is in place when it comes to external funding and media exposure while the criteria for extra or reduced research may be a bit flexible and take into consideration the personal situation of the individual. When it comes to the size of monetary rewards, we probably find the lowest level at department A. The highest level at a Danish university department is, however, not represented among the three examples. There are departments that reward their scholars for one top publication with up to €8,000.

Incentive Systems: Where and Why?[7]

There are substantial variations in how Danish university departments' use incentive systems to manage research performance and to what extent. What is more, a considerable number of departments do not use any type of system at all.

It is quite puzzling why these otherwise very similar organizational units differ so much with regard to the use of research performance incentive systems. According to *sociological institutionalism* (see Hall & Taylor 1996), we should expect the organizational forms and practices of organizations within the same organizational field[8] to become increasingly similar because the "organizations are driven to incorporate the practices and procedures defined by prevailing rationalized concepts of organizational work and institutionalized in society" (Meyer & Rowan 1977: 340). Organizations adopt what Røvik (1998) has labeled "institutionalized organizational recipes" independent of their immediate efficacy but in order to increase their legitimacy and appear as "modern organizations".[9] With regard to pay-for-performance, Park and Berry (2014) have described it as a successful diffusion of a failed policy.

The variations in the departments' use of incentive systems can be understood in a number of ways, however. Newer lines of research within sociological institutionalism has highlighted that organizations do not passively adopt "organizational recipes" but *translate* and adapt the (often broad and vague) concepts to the specific organizational context, culture, and identity (Czarniawska & Sevón 1996). Some have used the *virus* metaphor to explain how management ideas spread. Like viruses they are infectious, but there is an incubation period from when the host is exposed to the virus to when symptoms first appear, some hosts are immune to the disease, and the virus may mutate when it enters a new host (Røvik 2011). Other perspectives, on the other hand, give emphasis to the *rational* side of managerial decision-making (see Subramony 2006 for an overview). Moynihan (2005), for example, finds that the most important factor for explaining the implementation of performance management–inspired reforms is whether management believes in the management doctrine and whether they see it as a waste of time or an opportunity to be exploited.[10] The manager is said to do an approximate cost-benefit analysis based on the environmental conditions of his or her organization and internal organizational needs and capacities when deciding if and how to implement specific management concepts (Moynihan 2005: 232).

Elements of these different explanations all seem to be in play when we try to understand where and why research performance incentive systems are used in Danish university departments. A qualitative comparative fuzzy-set analysis (fsQCA) (see Ragin 2008) of the studied university departments identifies four "causal recipes" associated with the use of performance-related pay schemes to reward the individual researcher according to his or her research performance: (1) departments from outside the humanities where the chair believes that it is a good idea to reward scholars financially for publications; (2) teaching-intensive departments from outside the humanities where the dean uses financial incentives connected to the department's research performance; (3) large, teaching-intensive departments with low disagreement about the status attached to different types of publications; (4) large, research intensive departments where the dean uses financial incentives connected to the department's research performance (see Opstrup 2017).

The first of the four "causal recipes" has the highest coverage of the outcome and suggests that, outside the humanities, the department head's view of whether pecuniary incentives are a good way to motivate researchers to do research is important for the use of performance-based pay schemes. Of the studied departments only 3 of the 11 within the humanities (27 percent) "often" or "very often" reward researchers financially according to their research performance. The percentages are similar for departments within the natural and technical sciences and the health sciences; respectively, 23 and 22 percent "often" or "very often" use financial incentives. The social sciences, on the other hands, stand out. Here, 10 of the 17 departments (59 percent) "often" or "very often" reward research performance by bonuses or salary increases. Perhaps not so surprisingly, in particular, economics and business departments use financial incentives to manage research performance.

Also among the department heads there are mixed views about the usefulness of monetary rewards. In a survey of all Danish department heads,[11] 30 percent "totally" or "partly" agree that it is a good idea to reward researchers financially for publications in certain journals; 54 percent, however, "totally" or "partly" disagree. On the other hands, 66 percent "totally" or "partly" disagree with the statement "all other things being equal, you get the most productive environment if differences in pay only are based on position and seniority, not the individual researcher's research productivity"; 20 percent "totally" or "partly" agree.

In-depth analysis of interviews with department heads at the sampled departments helps us to understand the department heads somewhat contradicting positions towards the use of pay bonuses to reward the individual researcher's research performance. Three different comprehensions of what role financial incentives play for researchers' motivation can be identified. The interviewed department heads can be divided into "believers", "interpreters", and "non-believers" (see Opstrup 2017). As the name implies, "believers" believe that financial incentives have a positive impact on researchers' motivation and performance. On the other hand, "non-believers" do not believe in the use of financial rewards. Actually, they often think that they do more harm than good. Finally, the "interpreters" do not believe in the effect of the monetary reward in itself but trust that a bonus has symbolic value. It is the "pat on the back" and "the recognition of a job well done" that matters rather than the pecuniary reward. Among the chairs in the aforementioned fuzzy-set analysis, the "believer" position is the least frequent; 9 out of 40 (23 percent) can be categorized as "believers". Of the department heads, 12 (30 percent) are "non-believers", and the remaining 19 are categorized as "interpreters".

Thus, there are important differences between departments in the extent to which and why financial incentives are used to manage research performance and in how useful department heads view monetary rewards to motivate researchers. The design of specific incentive systems also varies between the departments where they are put to use (as previously discussed), thus indicating elements of "translation" or adaption to the local context.

Hypotheses

Under what circumstances do scholars tend to ignore the departmental control and reward systems? As mentioned earlier we generally expect that ignorance will be more widespread the less people have a chance to obtain rewards or to be hit by sanctions. In this respect we focus on the departmental control and reward regime in itself, more specifically four aspects of the regime: leadership attention, monitoring, use of economic rewards and the use of sanctions against underperformers. The indicators for regime are considered as characteristics of the department, i.e., as aggregated variables.

However, the regime characteristics are components in a larger causal system that includes a number of individual characteristics as well. In Figure 8.1 we have indicated the various hypothesized relations at different stages in the "funnel of causality" (see Campbell, Converse, Miller & Stokes 1960). The behavior we seek to explain, ignorance of control and reward systems, is a function of broader competencies, orientations, and dispositions like motivation and career expectations. These intervening factors are a function of more remote (or truly exogenous) factors such as gender, age, and tenure, characteristics of the departmental context in which the individual finds him or herself as well as attributes of the particular field of science.

In the figure we find three types of exogenous variables. First, the academic field (or branch of science) can be perceived as an "umbrella variable", covering a host of other factors like gender distribution, tenure, age, work composition grant performance, and motivation. Also, departmental characteristics may differ between the four branches of science. In the figure we make an effort to emphasize that the branch of science may be interpreted as an umbrella variable that covariate with these other factors. To the extent that we have been successful in identifying these factors, no remaining "effect" of the branch will be found in the final model. Or stated otherwise: to the extent that the academic field exhibits

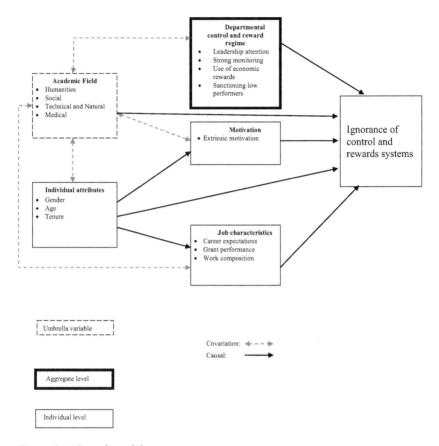

Figure 8.1 Causal model

a bivariate relationship with ignorance, we will interpret this as a spuri-
ous effect being the result of a *non-causal association* of academic field
with one or more of the other explanatory variable.

The second set of exogenous variables refers to individual attributes.
Gender, age, and tenure may affect ignorance via direct as well as indirect
paths. In both cases, we will talk about causal relations. The third set of
exogenous variables refers to the departmental level. These variables will
be interpreted the same way as the individual level variables, albeit with a
discussion of how macro characteristics may affect individual's attitudes.

The intervening variables, motivation, and job characteristics could
be considered dependent variables in their own right, in which case we
needed to figure out how they are related causally. For instance, it would
be obvious to assume that career expectations may be associated with
work composition. For the purpose of this chapter, we simply assume
that the intervening variables have the same position in the funnel of
causality with no causal relations existing between them.

We may also describe the relations in Figure 8.1 in the form of seven hypotheses, the first four of which imply a direction—positive or negative—of the causal relationship.

> Main hypothesis I: The stronger the control and reward regime of a department and the more it is monitored and enforced by the department chair the less it tends to be ignored by faculty members
>
> Hypothesis II: Extrinsically motivated scholars tend to exhibit lower levels of ignorance of control and reward systems
>
> Hypothesis III: The less promising the career prospect the more an individual tends to ignore control and reward systems
>
> Hypothesis IV: The more successful scholars are in terms of external grants the less they tend to ignore control and reward systems
>
> Hypothesis V: The academic field of faculty has important consequences for the level of ignorance of control and reward systems albeit via indirect effects only
>
> Hypothesis VI: Individual attributes like age, gender, and tenure are associated with the level of ignorance of control and reward systems
>
> Hypothesis VII: Work composition, i.e., time allocated for teaching, research, and administrative duties, is associated with the level of ignorance of control and reward systems

Design and Data

Our analysis of ignorance of control and reward systems is based on survey responses by scholars drawn from a sample of Danish university departments (see appendix). Rather than gathering observations from a simple cross section of researchers at Danish universities, the sample is defined in a two-stage sampling process designed to select researchers working in different types of departments reflecting as much variation as possible. The starting point is the population of 32 faculties[12] at the eight Danish universities with an average of five to six departments. In the first stage we have randomly selected 66 departments representing each and every faculty in Denmark. A minimum of two departments has been selected per faculty. In January 2011 all 4,984 academic employees (including Ph.D. students) at the selected departments were asked to fill out an online questionnaire focusing on publication strategies, coping behavior, motivation, incentives, organization and leadership, job situation etc. The overall response rate was 59.0 percent for academic staff in tenured or tenure-track positions (ranging from assistant professors/post docs to full professors).[13]

Since we are dealing with a hierarchical data structure (scholars are *nested* within departments), the analysis rests on multilevel regressions techniques. This methodology applies information at different levels in the same model, thus making it possible to assess the impact of departmental features on the individual researchers' degree of ignorance.

Measurement

Faculty members were asked two sets of questions regarding the existence and importance of monitoring and reward systems.

> *Danish university institutes/departments monitor and reward the research efforts of their staff in very different ways. Please indicate the extent to which the following methods are applied at your department.* (Response categories "yes", "no", or "don't know"):

> *The chair of the department can, to varying degrees, monitor and sanction or reward the research activity of staff members. Please indicate the degree to which the following methods are used in your department.* (Response categories "to very high degree", "to a high degree", "to some degree", "to a low degree", "not at all" and "don't know").

Two questions dealt with monitoring, two with leadership attention to research performance, three questions focused on low performers and the enforcement of sanctions, while three dealt with rewards in the form of one-time or permanent bonuses and the attraction of bonuses.

The responses are exhibited in Table 8.1. Looking first at the "yes"/"no" distributions and the index scores, there is a clear indication that monitoring and reward systems are not uniform phenomena experienced by Danish university scholars. Rather few departments seem to have control or reward systems; monitoring systems are more common; feedback from the chair is mainly something that takes place in connection with the periodic performance appraisals (typically yearly assessments). Few departments have explicit systems for rewarding high performers. All in all, incentive structures are only found sporadically at Danish universities.

A striking feature of Table 8.1 is the many "don't know" responses. Almost every scholar in Denmark is exposed to the annual assessments where he or she (typically) will meet his or her department chair. Nevertheless 18 percent do not know if research performance is a matter for discussion. One out of five faculty members do not know if there is a minimum quota for performance. One out of three does not know if low performers are penalized by reductions in their time for research. The same share does not know if there is a system that automatically links permanent salary increases to performance.

These distributions are based on the whole sample of scholars. Maybe they simply reflect that departments have different regimes in place, some clear, some ambiguous, or some non-existing. Or maybe they reflect differences in perceptions among individuals that are linked to career paths, motivation, or simply age?

The "don't know" responses are not scattered randomly among individuals. In order to investigate further this phenomenon, we have constructed

Table 8.1 Faculty member's perceptions of monitoring and incentive systems at Danish university departments

	Don't know	Yes	No	Index
1. Periodic monitoring of individuals' research publications is carried out, but the results are given only to the individual researcher.	24	21	55	
2. Periodic monitoring of individuals' research publications is carried out, and this is disseminated internally for the department.	17	39	44	
3. The chair of the department provides ongoing feedback to the individual researcher regarding their research and publications.	14			28
4. The individual staff member's research production is part of his or her periodic career development interview	18			60
5. The department has a minimum norm for how much the individual researcher is expected to publish.	21	37	43	
6. Researchers who do not publish enough have their research time reduced and are instead allocated additional tasks within teaching and administration.	35			24
7. The chair of the department is responsible for the research by calling faculty members who are not actively carrying out research activities.	42			48
8. The department has a system for automatic one-time bonus if one publishes in recognized journals.	18	3	80	
9. Permanent salary increases are given according to relatively known criteria connected to research publication.	33	11	56	
10. The salary bonuses awarded by my department are large enough that they in fact are worth pursuing.	32			26

Note: N = 1,599 (max) to 1,571 (min). The index score takes values from 0 (not at all) to 100 (to a very high degree).

a measure of *ignorance* which simply counts the number of "don't know"s across the ten items for each individual respondent and multiply by 10.[14] Our measure of ignorance thus takes values from 0–100. The average score for all respondents is 22.2. There are rather small differences across the four main fields of science with a tendency for the social science to score a bit lower than the other field (social science: 20.2; medicine 24.2; the humanities: 25.5; and natural and technical sciences: 26.3). Across universities the differences seem to be slightly larger with a high for one of the old universities at 25.3 and the lowest score for one of the new universities at 12.4.[15] However, there are huge differences between departments, even

Table 8.2 Independent variables

		Mean	St. dev.
Field of science (based on department)			
Humanities	1 if humanities, 0 otherwise	0.214	
Social science (reference group in regressions)	1 if social science, 0 otherwise	0.202	
Technical and natural science	1 if technical/natural science, 0 otherwise	0.440	
Medical science	1 if medical science, 0 otherwise	0.145	
Individual attributes			
Female	1 if female, 0 if male	0.320	
Age	Respondents age in years	46.2	10.9
Tenure	1 if tenure position, 0 otherwise	0.691	
Departmental control and reward regime[1]			
Leadership attention	Additive index, items 3, 4, 6, and 7 in Table 8.1	37.2	10.9
Strong monitoring	Additive index, items 1 and 2 in table 8.1	59.8	19.9
Use of economic rewards	Additive index, items 8 and 9 in Table 8.1	15.4	19.9
Minimum norms for research performance	Value item 5 in Table 8.1	34.7	26.8
Motivation			
Extrinsic motivation	See text below, 0–100 scale	53.2	19.6
Job characteristics			
Career expectations	1 if already full professor, 0 otherwise	0.20	
	1 if next step on career ladder is perceived as certain, 0 otherwise	0.28	
	1 if advancement seems unlikely or given up, 0 otherwise	0.35	
Work composition (self-reported)			
	Weekly hours spend on teaching	13.6	9.4
	Weekly hours spend on research	17.5	9.7
	Weekly hours spend on administration	6.8	6.8
Grant performance	Number of external grants received within the last three years	1.2	1.5

[1] The variables for "Departmental control and reward regime" are based on a factor analysis of the ten items in Table 8.1 (item 10 in Table 8.1 did not load on any factor). Scores are average score for all respondents in each department. Means and standard deviations based on department ($N = 66$) as unit of analysis.

Source: Extrinsic motivation

The measurement of the motivational structure of faculty members is based on the following question:

If you consider the ideal job, how important do you find the following attributes?

Eight job attributes were mentioned[1] with five response categories: "very important", "important", "less important", "unimportant", "very unimportant". The most important attributes of the ideal job of a Danish university scholar are freedom and independence, to work on the front line of research and opportunities for professional and personal development, all attributes that are inherently part of an intrinsic motivational structure. When adding to this list the slightly less important "peer recognition of high-quality research", we have in front of us the four items which load strongly on the second dimension of the ensuing factor analysis's second dimension.[2] The three least important job attributes are connected to salaries, material benefits, financial rewards, and career opportunities, which load heavily on the first factor and can obviously be labeled "extrinsically motivated". An additive index was calculated based on the three job attributes standardized to a 0–100 scale.

[1] Four of the eight attributes were taken from well-known standard questions in the motivation literature while four were developed with special reference to the job of a university scholar.

[2] The factor analysis of the eight job attributes produced two dimensions with eigenvalues larger than 1 (2.56 and 1.34, respectively).

at the same university and same faculty. One of the science departments at university X thus exhibits an ignorance score of 39.5, while a social science department from the same university stands at 8.8. These are the highest and lowest scores among our sample of departments. Based on intensive interviews with the two chairs we find that both departments only "rarely" pay for research performance. These findings indicate that faculties and departments have quite different practices when it comes to control and reward systems.

The measurement of the independent variables is exhibited in Table 8.2.

Analysis

Our main hypothesis stated that the strength of the control and reward system as well as monitoring and enforcement efforts by the department chair would affect the level of ignorance among faculty members. Generally, this hypothesis did not find strong support in our analyses (see Table 8.3) as three out of the four factors seem to be unimportant for the level of ignorance.

Leadership attention was measured by the following three items:

- feedback from the chair to individual researchers about their research and publications,
- the inclusion of research production in the regular career development interviews (job appraisals), reallocation of tasks for low performers, and
- taking responsibility to react towards so-called zero-researchers.

Table 8.3 Explaining Danish university scholars' ignorance of control and reward systems (multilevel regression [standardized coefficients])

	Model 1	Model 2	Model 3	Model 4	Model 5	Model 6
Aggregate level						
Field of science						
Humanities	0.12**			0.06		0.04
	(0.03)			(0.04)		(0.03)
Natural and technical sciences	0.13**			0.07		0.05
	(0.04)			(0.04)		(0.04)
Medical and health sciences	0.07**			0.02		0.04
	(0.04)			(0.03)		(0.03)
Departments control and reward regimes						
Leadership attention		0.01		0.00		0.01
		(0.03)		(0.03)		(0.03)
Strong monitoring system		-0.09**		-0.09**		-0.08**
		(0.03)		(0.03)		(0.03)
Use of economic rewards		-0.07*		-0.04		-0.04
		(0.03)		(0.03)		(0.03)
Minimum norms for publications		-0.05		-0.03		-0.03
		(0.03)		(0.03)		(0.03)
Individual level						
Individual attributes						
Female			0.11**	0.11**		0.10**
			(0.02)	(0.02)		(0.02)
Age (ln)			-0.06+	-0.06+		-0.08**
			(0.03)	(0.03)		(0.03)
Tenure			-0.33**	-0.32**		-0.22**
			(0.03)	(0.03)		(0.03)
Motivation						
Extrinsic motivation					-0.03	-0.06**
					(0.02)	(0.02)

	(1)	(2)	(3)	(4)	(5)	(6)
Career expectations						
Sure or almost sure about advancement					0.07* (0.03)	-0.03 (0.03)
Given up or pessimistic about advancement					0.23** (0.03)	0.11** (0.03)
Work composition						
Hours spent on teaching					-0.11** (0.03)	-0.03 (0.03)
Hours spent on research					0.10** (0.03)	0.07** (0.03)
Hours spent on administration					-0.15** (0.03)	-0.08** (0.03)
Grant performance						
Number of grants obtained					-0.14** (0.03)	-0.11** (0.03)
Pseudo R^2 (department level)	0.23	0.01	0.22	0.91	0.64	0.93
Pseudo R^2 (individual level)	0.02	0.36	0.16	0.16	0.97	0.21
N (departments)	66	66	66	66	66	66
N (individuals)	1,438	1,438	1,438	1,438	1,438	1,438

$+ p < 0.10$, $* p < 0.05$, $** p < 0.01$ (standard errors in parentheses)

According to our analyses, there is no indication that leadership attention has any bearing upon an individual's overall degree of ignorance about the control and reward systems at his or her department.

The second factor without any significant effect on ignorance is the use of minimum norms for publication. Finally, the use of economic rewards for research publications in the form of one-time bonuses or permanent salary increases also did not affect the level of ignorance.

The only significant effect on ignorance seems to stem from monitoring which is a composite measure based on two items about periodic monitoring of research publications with individual and collective feedback. The existence of monitoring seems to be a rather strong predictor of ignorance, which is independent of model specification.

The importance of control and reward regimes in other words seem to be concentrated in one dimension. Strong monitoring systems tend to lead to lower level of ignorance while the existence of minimum norms for research performance, leadership attention, and use of economic rewards seem to be unimportant.

Looking at column 1 there are clear differences across the four fields of science. Faculty from the reference category, the social sciences, is significantly less ignorant than scholars from the other branches. In the final model, there are no differences between the four branches of science, confirming the expectation that field of science is merely an umbrella variable (hypothesis V confirmed). More in-depth analyses (not reported here) show that this is due to different control and reward regimes across the four fields, particularly a preference for use of economic rewards within the social sciences.

The bivariate "effect" of the field of science is not due to differences in the gender, age, or tenure distribution across the four fields, despite the fact that gender has a direct effect in the full model. Female scholars tend to be more ignorant than males, older faculty members tend to be less ignorant than young colleagues while tenured faculty exhibit a very low level of ignorance compared to non-tenured. Tenure is by far the most important predictor of ignorance (hypothesis VI is confirmed).

The level of ignorance is—not surprisingly—associated with motivational structure. The more extrinsically motivated a person is, the less ignorant he or she usually is about the control and reward system at his or her department (hypothesis II is confirmed). The way university scholars think about their future careers also affects their level of ignorance. Scholars who have given up or who are pessimistic about future advancement seem to be the most ignorant compared to full professors (reference group). On the other hand, people who feel sure or almost sure of climbing to the next step on the career ladder are less ignorant than the reference group (hypothesis III is confirmed).

The second most important explanatory factor is work composition, cf. the combined coefficients for hours spent on teaching, research, and administration.[16] Higher activity in the research field is associated with higher levels of ignorance. On the other hand, faculty members who spend much time on administration tend to know more about control and reward systems (hypothesis VII is confirmed). Finally, hypothesis IV is also confirmed: the more successful a faculty member is in terms of obtaining external research grants, the more he or she tends to know about the departmental control and reward system.

Conclusions

A performance-based regime rewarding good (or plenty!) research or punishing underperformers is based on a set of criteria defining rewards and penalties for certain forms of behavior. Behavior is monitored by management, individual performance is appraised against the criteria, and rewards and penalties are handed out accordingly. Employees will know the rules of the game and act accordingly: desired behavior—as determined by the principal—will come to dominate and unwanted performance will be reduced. Proponents of performance management assume that the selfish agent knows the rules and, if the system is set up in a clever way, he or she will do everything to meet the preferences of the principal. Skeptics similarly assume that the selfish agent knows the rules and will do everything he or she can to circumvent them while at the same time meeting the targets. Is this common assumption true in the real world of universities?

The answer is no.

We have investigated the level of ignorance (the opposite of knowledge) of faculty members about the control and rewards regimes at their department. The indicator of ignorance can take values from 0 to 100. Among Danish universities the lowest score is 12 and the highest 25. Among departments actual scores lie between a low of 9 and a high of 40. A striking feature of the multivariate analysis is that the actual nature of the control and reward regime has very little bearing on the level of ignorance. Among the four regime dimensions only one, the monitoring system, seems to affect the level of ignorance among faculty members. This result corresponds to the observation that many departments seem to apply broad, diffuse, and ambiguous rules and procedures for rewarding and penalizing employees with discretionary power resting with the chairs. Thereby management is able to react according to the situation at hand and make sure that not only research but also other vital functions resting at a department may be taken into account when favors are distributed.

Another major finding is that research active, tenured, successful, externally motivated, and hopeful (for advancement) faculty members exhibit lower levels of ignorance than scholars who have a bleak view of their future career, and put a relatively large number of hours into other activities than research and who are internally motivated.

Non-tenured faculty—assistant professors and postdocs—display a rather high level of ignorance about the departmental control and reward regimes, a reflection of their short time of experiences with the system, but this is most likely because their focus is on another incentive system, which will bring them the most attractive reward, the tenured associate professorship.

Finally, one notices that women seem to be more ignorant than men. Several explanations may be given for this difference, like a different work composition, a more pessimistic view of chances for career advancement, years of experience or motivational structure. However, these factors are exactly the ones that have been controlled for, still leaving gender with a relatively strong direct effect on ignorance.

Notes

1. One could assume that the local shop steward will always represent the applicant and seek the largest possible remuneration, while management will have a firm grip on the wallet. This is definitely a wrong assumption. The local union representative often acts out of notions of fairness and equal pay to everyone and will often prefer more jobs to higher salaries.
2. It was not possible to categorize 3 of the 66 departments in the sample.
3. Here we focus solely on one-time bonuses. Each department has a similar system for the release of permanent salary increases that correspond to the system for one-time bonuses.
4. All amounts mentioned in this section has been rounded to nearest hundred.
5. These are "examples", but it is no coincidence that the examples are solely focused on research. No bonuses for teaching, development, community service, and the like are mentioned in the criteria for one-time bonuses. Extra efforts within those fields may however be taken into consideration when it comes to permanent increases.
6. This scheme, which was is university wide, operating with three levels of remuneration, has recently been abolished.
7. This section is partly based on Opstrup (2017).
8. Organizational fields are defined as organizations that in the aggregate constitute a recognized area of institutional life; for example, organizations that produce similar services and products (DiMaggio & Powell 1983: 148).
9. Three types of institutional pressures (coercive, normative, and mimetic) cause organizations to adopt the same practices and procedures and become *isomorphic*. Coercive isomorphism results from formal and informal pressures from other organizations which the organization in some way is dependent upon; normative isomorphism stems from norms and practices diffused through the formal education and the professional networks of managers and practitioners within the field; while mimetic isomorphism is caused by uncertainty about what is the proper organizational form. This uncertainty encourages the organization to imitate the organizational practices of successful organizations within the field (DiMaggio & Powell 1991).
10. More specifically, Moynihan (2005) studied the implementation of performance information systems in three different U.S. state governments.
11. All 179 department heads at Danish universities were surveyed in Winter 2010/2011. In total, 128 (72 percent) answered the questionnaire.
12. At the four universities, RUC, DTU, CBS, and ITU, there is no level between the vice-chancellor and the individual department. These universities are considered as faculties when it comes to sampling.

13. Ph.D. students are not included in the present analysis. The response rate for this group was considerably lower, 44.6 percent.
14. Cronbach's alpha for all ten items (dummies for "don't know") is 0.824.
15. If we rank the departments according to the average "don't know" answers across all ten items, six universities are represented among the seven lowest ranked departments. At the others end of the ranking six universities are represented among the 12 highest don't know shares.
16. One could have expected a multicollinearity problem in this context since time allocation for the three main functions of a university scholar, teaching, research, and administration, necessarily will be negatively related. This is not the case, however.

References

Andersen, L.B. & Pallesen, T. 2008, "Not Just for the Money? How Financial Incentives Affect the Number of Publications at Danish Research Institutions", *International Public Management Journal*, vol. 11, no. 1, pp. 28–47.

Andersen, L.B., Eriksson, T., Kristensen, N. & Pedersen, L.H. 2012, "Attracting Public Service Motivated Employees: How to Design Compensation Packages", *International Review of Administrative Sciences*, vol. 78, no. 4, pp. 615–641.

Barzelay, M. 2001, *New Public Management*, University of California Press, Berkeley.

Bevan, G. & Hood C. 2006, "What Get Measured Is What Matters. Targets and Gaming in the English Public Health Care System," *Public Administration*, vol. 84, no. 3, pp. 517–538.

Czarniawska, B. & Sevón, G., eds. 1996, *Translating Organizational Change*, Walter de Gruyter, Berlin.

Campbell, A., Converse, P.E., Miller, W.E. & Stokes, D.E. 1960, *The American Voter*, University of Chicago Press, Chicago.

de Bruijn, H. 2007, *Managing Performance in the Public Sector*, Routledge, New York.

DiMaggio, P.J. & Powell W.W. 1983, "The Iron Cage Revisited: Institutional Isomorphism and Collective Rationality in Organizational Fields", *American Sociological Review*, vol. 48, no. 2, pp. 147–160.

DiMaggio, P.J. & Powell, W.W. 1991, "The Iron Cage Revisited: Institutional Isomorphism and Collective Rationality", in *The New Institutionalism in Organizational Analysis*, eds. W. W. Powell & P. J. DiMaggio, The University of Chicago Press, Chicago.

Frey, B.S. 1997, Not Just for the Money: An Economic Theory of Personal Motivation, Edward Elgar Publishing Inc, Northampton.

Frey, B.S. 2003, "Publishing as Prostitution?—Choosing Between One's Own Ideas and Academic Success", *Public Choice*, vol. 116, no. 1–2, pp. 205–223.

Frey, B.S. & Jegen, R. 2001, "Motivation Crowding Theory", *Journal of Economic Surveys*, vol. 15, no. 5, pp. 589–610.

Frey, B.S. & Oberholzer-Gee, F. 1997, "The Cost of Price Incentives: An Empirical Analysis of Motivation Crowding- Out", *The American Economic Review*, vol. 87, no. 4, pp. 746–755.

Gillies, D. 2008, *How Should Research be Organised?* College Publications, London.

Hall, P.A. & Taylor, R. 1996, "Political Science and the Three New Institutionalisms", *Political Studies*, vol. 44, no. 5, pp. 936–957.

Hicks, D. 2012, "Performance-based Research Funding Systems", *Research Policy*, vol. 41, pp. 251–261.

Jacobsen, C.B. & Andersen, L.B. 2014, "Performance Management for Academic Researchers: How Publication Command Systems Affect Individual Behavior", *Review of Public Personnel Administration*, vol. 34, no. 2, pp. 84–107.

Lepper, M.R. & Greene, D. 1978, *The Hidden Costs of Reward: New Perspectives on the Psychology of Human Motivation*, L. Erlbaum Associates, New York.

Meyer, J.W. & Rowan, B. 1977, "Institutionalized Organizations: Formal Structure as Myth and Ceremony". *The American Journal of Sociology*, vol. 83, no. 2, pp. 340–363.

Miller, G. J. 2005, "The Political Evolution of Principal-Agent Models". *Annual Review of Political Science*, vol. 8, pp. 203–225.

Moynihan, D. 2005, "Why and How Do State Governments Adopt and Implement "Managing for Results" Reforms?", *Journal of Public Administration Research and Theory*, vol. 15, no. 2, pp. 219–243.

Mouritzen, P.E. & Opstrup, N. 2019, *Performance Management at Universities: The Danish Bibliometric Research Indicator at Work*, University of Southern Denmark Press, Odense.

OECD. 2010, *Performance-based Funding for Public Research in Tertiary Education Institutions: Workshop Proceedings*, OECD Publishing, Paris.

Opstrup, N. 2017, "When and Why Do University Managers Use Publication Incentive Payments?", *Journal of Higher Education Policy and Management*, vol. 39, no. 5, pp. 524–539.

Osterloh, M. 2010, "Governance by Numbers. Does It Really Work in Research?", *Analyse & Kritik*, vol. 2, pp. 267–283.

Park, S. & Berry, F. 2014, "Successful Diffusion of a Failed Policy. The Case of Pay-For-Performance in the US Federal Government", *Public Management Review*, vol. 16, no. 6, pp. 763–781.

Radin, B. 2006, *Challenging the Performance Movement Accountability, Complexity, and Democratic Values*, Georgetown University Press, Washington DC.

Ragin, C.C. 2008, *Redesigning Social Inquiry. Fuzzy Sets and Beyond*, University of Chicago Press, Chicago.

Røvik, K.A. 1998, *Moderne organisasjoner - Trender i organisasjonstenkningen ved tusenårsskiftet*, Fagbokforlaget, Oslo.

Røvik, K.A. 2011, "From Fashion to Virus: An Alternative Theory of Organizations' Handling of Management Ideas", *Organizational Studies*, vol. 32, no. 5, pp. 631–653.

Skinner, B. F., 1953, *Science and Human Behavior*, Free Press, New York.

Smith, P. 1995, "On the Unintended Consequences of Publishing Performance Data in the Public Sector", *International Journal of Public Administration*, vol. 18, no. 2–3, pp. 277–310.

Stajkovic, A. D. & F. Luthans 1997, "A Meta-Analysis of the Effects of Organizational Behavior Modification on Task Performance", *Academy of Management Journal*, vol. 40, no. 5, pp. 1122–1149.

Steel, P. & C. J. König 2006, "Integrating Theories of Work Motivation". *Academy of Management Review*, vol. 31, no. 4, pp. 889–913.

Subramony, M. 2006, "Why Organizations Adopt Some Human Resource Management Practices and Reject Others: An Exploration of Rationales", *Human Resource Management*, vol. 45, no. 2, pp. 195–210.

Swiss, J. E. 2005, "A Framework for Assessing Incentives in Results-Based Management", *Public Administration Review*, vol. 65, no. 5, pp. 592–602.

van Thiel, S. & Leeuw, F.L. 2002, "The Performance Paradox in the Public Sector". *Public Performance and Management Review*, vol. 25, no. 3, pp. 267–281.

Vroom, V. H. 1964, *Work and Motivation*, Wiley, New York.

Weibel, A., Rost, K. & Osterloh, M. 2010, "Pay for Performance in the Public Sector—Benefits and (Hidden) Costs", *Journal of Public Administration Research and Theory*, vol. 20, no. 2, pp. 387–412.

Weingart, P. 2005, "Impact of Bibliometrics Upon the Science System: Inadvertent Consequences?" *Scientometrics*, vol. 62, no. 1, pp. 117–131.

9 Modern Management and Working Conditions in Academia

Signe Pihl-Thingvad and Niels Opstrup

Introduction

Universities have gone through significant changes the past two decades. In Denmark as well as other countries, a wide range of new ways of governing universities and managing academics have been introduced based on New Public Management (NPM) and different *performance management* principles (Kristensen, Nøreklit & Raffnsøe-Møller 2011).

In its essence, performance management practices are intended to improve the performance of public organizations, moving focus from traditional input- and process-orientated management to base decisions and controls on output and outcomes (Moynihan 2008). Central management practices often highlighted with regard to performance management are setting clear organizational goals, measuring/monitoring (organizational) performance against these goals, and in different ways providing public organizations or (individual) public employees with incentives to focus on results and improve performance (see, e.g., Pollitt 2013).

On the microlevel, these management practices are expected to regulate the behavior of the employees by affecting their reactions and attitudes to work. Performance management has been associated with positive employee attitudes such as increased motivation, job satisfaction, and organizational commitment (Yang & Kassekert 2010; Yang & Pandey 2009; Fletcher & Williams 1996). Goal-setting theory (Locke & Latham 2002) argues that setting clear organizational goals may have a motivating effect (at least if the goals are accepted among the employees in the organization) (Latham, Borgogni & Pettita 2008). Likewise, measuring or monitoring performance may also motivate employees if it is used to provide a sense of accomplishment towards reaching significant organizational goals (Behn 2003) Finally, incentives (either positive or negative, budgetary or pecuniary, verbal or symbolic) is per se intended to provide organizations or employees with the motivation to pay attention to results and better performance (Swiss 2005). In this way, the management tools are designed to enhance positive reactions to work and thereby increase employees' performance.

To implement this motivational strategy, an agency's leadership needs to give its people a significant goal to achieve and then use performance measures—including interim targets—to focus people's thinking and work and to provide a periodic sense of accomplishment.

However, the increased focus on results and outputs can also create too much pressure to perform and may function as a stressor instead (Sewel et al. 2012; Mather & Seifert 2011). Furthermore, if the performance measures are unclear or the management practices are clashing with the existing organizational culture, then it may lead to frustration and a loss of meaning in work (Moynihan 2009: 594). If employees experience frustrations or dissatisfaction and associate that with the performance management tools, there will be greater risk that they react with either passive or even counterproductive responses. In such situations, performance management is unlikely to improve (organizational or individual) performance, but may cause perverse effects instead (Moynihan 2009: 596).

Still, our empirical knowledge of employees' reactions to performance management is sparse and there is a need for more research on the relationship between the use of performance management practices and the employees' perception of their psychosocial work environment and their stress levels (Noblet et al. 2006: 352). In this regard universities are an interesting case, since performance routines within a shorter period has become a central institutional influence and have been implemented in a strong Humboldtian organizational culture which may clash with some of the principles underlying performance management. The new performance management routines are expected to impact on the employees' psychosocial work environment, but we do not know if management's practices support the employees' reactions to work by increasing their motivation and satisfaction with work or if, on the contrary, it challenges their perception of work and cause frustration or even stress.

We address this knowledge gap by analyzing how the use of five different performance management practices at Danish university departments are associated with (1) the nested researchers' satisfaction with the psychosocial work environment and (2) their perceptions of stress.

In this way this chapter contributes with an analysis on the microlevel of the relationship between the implemented management practices at the universities and the researchers' reactions. The results might help us to get a better understanding of why the reformed management systems do and do not reach its intended effects at the universities. Furthermore, we investigate these mechanisms over time to see if there are any indications that the new management practices have reshaped the researchers' reactions to work in a more fundamental way.

In the following section, we elaborate on the concept of performance management. Next, we discuss how performance management practices can be expected to relate to the psychosocial work environment and stress. Then, data, measures, and methods are presented. This is followed by a presentation of the results. Finally, we conclude by discussing the practical and theoretical implications of our findings.

Performance Management in the Public Sector

Performance management is a subset of the wider NPM doctrine (Moynihan 2008). At its most general, performance management is a set of arguments about how core public services can be managed more effectively and improve the performance of public organizations. It goes under different names (such as *managing for results* [Moynihan 2006], *management by objectives and results* [Christensen, Lægreid & Stigen 2006], *outcomes-based performance management* [Heinrich 2002], or *result-based management* [Swiss 2005]), it is defined in a variety of ways, and it highlights and emphasizes an array of constituting parts and specific management practices. In all cases, however, the intention is to improve the performance of public organizations by "moving focus from process-oriented and rule-driven management to performance-orientated and result-driven management" (Behn 2016: 6).

Walker, Boyne, and Brewer (2010) point out that performance management is generally seen as involving setting clear organizational goals, operationalizing the goals to targets on relevant indicators, evaluating goal attainment on the basis of these indicators, and taking corrective actions based on the performance information when required. Pollitt (2013) similarly outlines the core logic as including setting objectives, deriving measurable targets from the objectives, and deploying a wide variety of instruments of authority or incentive that encourage staff to hit or exceed their targets. Among the essentials of the performance management doctrine that Ammons and Roenigk (2015) highlight are these: goal clarity, emphasis on results rather than on inputs and procedural compliance, performance monitoring/measurement, increased autonomy and flexibility at decentralized levels coupled with accountability for results, and incentives and possibly sanctions tied to performance results.

In the analysis, we examine how the use of five different performance management practices at Danish university departments are associated with the nested researchers' satisfaction with the psychosocial work environment and their perceptions of stress. These five are these: (1) setting clear organizational goals, (2) monitoring (publication) performance, (3) minimum performance standards, (4) financial incentives, and (5) sanctions.

We compare the relationships between the performance management practices and the researchers' reactions to their work in two cross-sectional datasets from 2011 and 2015.

Moynihan (2009) discusses how performance management systems may have both first-order and second-order effects. First-order effects are effects of performance management on organizational performance information use mediated by different relevant individual and organizational variables, for example the organizational culture (Moynihan

2009) or the employees' psychosocial work environment (Opstrup & Pihl-Thingvad 2018). Second-order effects describe the situations where the performance management practices have reshaped the mediating variable themselves and thereby, over time, have changed for example the employees' general perception of their work environment.

> Both types of effects reflect how performance routines interact with other important variables. But first-order effects are usually indicative of the short-term impact of new reforms. Second order effects will become more pronounced if and when performance routines become a central institutional influence.
>
> (Moynihan 2009: 597)

Second-order effects are likely to occur over time or if governance mechanisms have been radically reorganized to make performance routines dominant (Moynihan 2009: 597). The reform from 2007 in the Danish university sector did reorganize the governance system based on a range of dominant performance management practices, and furthermore the introduction of the bibliometric system in 2010 lay a national ground for comparing researchers' performance across the universities. Therefore, it is interesting to examine if these management practices impact on the employees' perception of their psychosocial work environment and thereby create second-order effects. Existing research provides most information about first-order effects (Moynihan 2009: 601). However,

> By focusing on broader long-term impacts, the hypotheses on second order effects are necessarily more speculative. . . . While modelling first-order effects is perhaps more traceable, examining second-order effects is the more important long-term challenge and ultimate indicator of how results-based reforms have affected governance.
>
> (Moynihan 2009: 601)

By comparing the results from 2011 and 2015 we may get indications of possible long-term impacts of the reformed governance system at Danish universities. We argue that the employees' perception of the different management tools may reshape their overall perception of their psychosocial work environment over time and thereby reconstitute their reactions to their work situation in general.

Performance Management and Psychosocial Working Conditions

By psychosocial work environment we mean the employees' psychological perception of (and interaction with) the characteristics of the workplace (Schbracq, Winnubst & Cooper 2003).

There are a range of different important dimensions influencing the psychosocial work environment, for example the content and organization of the work, demands in work, interpersonal relationships in work, conflicts in work and employees' reactions to their work situation (Kristensen, Hannerz, Hogh & Borg 2005; Pejtersen, Kristensen, Borg & Bjørner 2010; Clausen, Madsen, Christensen et al. 2017). In this chapter we focus on the employees' reactions to their work situation (Clausen, Madsen, Christensen et al. 2017)—which, in our opinion, is the most relevant dimension of the psychosocial work environment—when we consider employees' reactions to performance management. This dimension focuses on several types of reactions among employees. Beside the employees' overall satisfaction with their psychosocial work environment, it includes the employees' perception of meaning in their work, their commitment in work, their engagement in work, their perception of insecurity in work, their self-reported stress, their job satisfaction, and their perceptions of work-life balance. These types of reactions are considered among the most important reactions to the employees' work situation and thus to their psychosocial work environment (Clausen, Madsen, Christensen et al. 2017: 19). To examine both positive and negative reactions in the psychosocial work environment, we have chosen to focus on the employees' self-reported satisfaction with their psychosocial work environment and their perception of work-related stress.

Overall, research has shown that if employees are satisfied with their work, they will also be more positive towards organizational changes (for example related to larger reforms) and they will be more willing to experiment with and implement new ways of working (Wulandari, Mangundjaya, & Utoyo 2015). Research has also shown that if employees perceive their psychosocial work environment as overall satisfying, they might also be more likely to use performance information in a purposeful way in the organization (Fletcher & Williams 1996). Furthermore, the different performance management tools may impact the employees' satisfaction with their psychosocial work environment. For example, has several studies have shown that setting clear organizational goals is correlated with positive affective responses from the employees and higher satisfaction with their psychosocial work environment (Locke & Latham 1990, 2011; Wright 2004, 2007; Chun & Rainey 2005; Rainey & Rhu 2004). Using incentives may also be important for employees' psychosocial work environment. Incentives are expected to motivate employees to improve performance. Siegrist has pointed out that employees need to perceive a balance between their effort and the organizational rewards to be satisfied with their psychosocial work environment (Siegrist 2012). But empirical studies on the effect of rewards and sanctions as motivators in the public sector show inconsistent results (Jacobsen 2012). Furthermore, Siegrist also argues that if there is an imbalance between the employees' perception of their effort and the rewards, on the contrary, it will lead to stress (Siegrist 1996).

Thus the performance management tools may also lead to stress depending on the implementation of the tools and the employees' perception of the tools. For example, the visibility performance management induces related to the results and individual performance is often discussed as a positive factor in the theories (e.g., Forrester 2011). However, the appraisal identities both good and bad performers. But the emphasis in the literature is rarely on those cases where visibility reveals the inadequate or poor performance even though identifying these is of course just as great a part of the idea behind performance management. Therefore, performance appraisals can be uncomfortable for some employees (Lawler et al. 2012). Furthermore, from early on, Pollitt (1990) noted that PM was received with demoralization, resentment, and suspicion among the employees (Pollitt 1990: 178). Recent studies, likewise, show that employees perceived performance measurement as unfair and coercive (Sewell et al. 2012) and as an instrument of greater control and surveillance (Forrester 2011). Other empirical studies have also showed ambiguous results concerning the employees' reactions to performance management. Research has linked performance practices to perceptions of unjustness (Kick et al. 2006), increased job turn-over intensions (Lee & Jimenez 2011), and perceptions of higher intrusiveness, oppressiveness, and surveillance (Sewel et al. 2012), as well as reflecting mistrust toward the employees (Le Grand 2010; Christensen, Lægreid & Stigen 2007). Furthermore, Korunka et al. (2003) has shown that NPM in general was accompanied by increased job strain and at the same time mixed results in job satisfaction. Similarly, Noblet et al. (2006) identified several organization-specific stressors that characterized the NPM environment. This led the researchers to conclude that "the profound changes occurring in the public sector under the rubric of NPM are resulting in increased levels of stress for workers" (Noblet et al. 2006: 352).

Thus, it seems that PM is related to two different and partly opposing outcomes with regard to psychosocial work environment variables. However, empirical knowledge of the relationship between PM and the psychosocial work environment is still sparse. A closer understanding of the targeted employees' affective responses is important since they are likely to determine if performance management practices actually improve performance in the organizations or lead to unintended negative consequences instead.

Data and Measurement

We make use of the two surveys of Danish university researchers presented in Chapter 2 to examine the relationship between university departments' use of performance management practices and the nested researchers' satisfaction with the psychosocial work environment and their perceptions of stress.

Dependent Variables

The measure for our first dependent variable, satisfaction with the psychosocial work environment is measured by this question:

> Concerning your job in general, how satisfied are you with your psychosocial work environment? By psychosocial work environment, we mean, for example, the social climate, relations with management, demands on your work, your work time, your influence on your work, etc.

Response categories range from "very dissatisfied" (0) to "very satisfied" (100).

The measure is taken from the Copenhagen Psychosocial Questionnaire (COPSOQ) (see www.copsoq-network.org). The question is used as a global measure of employees' perception of their psychosocial work environment and has been shown to correlate with all dimensions included in the category "employees' reactions to their psychosocial work environment" in the expected directions (Clausen et al. 2017: 267). It has also been validated against a broader range of questions and indexes and all existing tests of the item support that it is a good proxy measure for the employees' psychosocial work environment (ibid.).

Our second dependent variable, the researchers' perceptions of stress, is measured by the question: "Stress is considered a situation in which one feels tense, restless, nervous or anxious or cannot sleep at night because you think about the problems all the time. Do you presently feel this kind of stress?" Options range from "not at all" (0) to "very much" (100).

The question has been applied and tested in several studies, and Elo et al. (2003) have demonstrated that it is a valid measure to reach conclusions at group levels about mental well-being.

Independent Variables

We also use answers from the surveyed researchers to measure the departments' use of performance management practices. However, because evaluations of management can be influenced by the satisfaction with the psychosocial work environment and level of stress, we use aggregated department means to get a more objective measures of the departments' management practices.

In the survey, the researchers were asked a number of questions regarding the management at their department and the existence and importance of monitoring and reward systems. From these questions, we construct measures for the departments' use of performance management practices.

The degree to which management formulate clear organizational goals is measured by each department's mean score on the question: "The department has clear goals and a strategy for how to reach those goals" (response categories range from "strongly disagree" [0] to "strongly agree" [100]).

Performance monitoring is measured based on the percentage of researchers who indicate the following: "Periodically (possibly once a year) a complete tabulation of the staff's research publications is carried out" at the department (options were "yes", "no", or "don't know").

In similar way, a measure for minimum performance standards is created based on the percentage of researchers who indicate that the following: "The department has a minimum quota for how much the individual researcher is expected to publish" (options were again "yes", "no", or "don't know").[1]

Measures of incentives is included as both rewards and sanctions. The department's use of individual financial rewards is measured based on the percentage of researchers who indicate the following: "The department has a system for giving an automatic one-time bonus if one publishes in the recognized journals" and whether "Qualification bonuses (permanent salary bonuses) are distributed according to relatively known criteria connected to research publication" (in both cases the possible options were "yes", "no", or "don't know"). The use of sanctions is measured by the aggregate mean for the department to the question: "Researchers who do not publish enough have their research time reduced and are instead allocated additional tasks within teaching and administration" (response categories range from "not at all" [0] to "to a very high degree" [100]).

Control Variables

Several studies describe how variations in the perception of the psychosocial work environment and stress levels among Danish university researchers are influenced by individual factors such as age, gender, position in the system, perception of career/opportunities, and general working conditions (see Clarke et al. 2012; Wright 2011; Krejsler 2011). Therefore, we include measures for age, gender, age career-level, perceived possibilities for advancement, average weekly working hours (self-reported), percentage of time used on research in an average week (self-reported), and main area of research (humanities, social sciences, natural and technical sciences or medical and health sciences).

Table 9.1 provides descriptive statistics for all the included variables in as well 2011 and 2015.

Estimation

Since our data include both organizational measures and measures at the level of the individual (nested) researchers, we apply multilevel regressions techniques in order to avoid ecological and atomistic fallacies (Hox

Table 9.1 Summary of included variables

	2011		2015	
	Mean	Std. dev.	Mean	Std. dev.
Dependent variables				
Satisfaction with the psychosocial work environment	65.55	25.73	64.87	26.47
Perceptions of stress	33.44	32.18	33.14	33.19
Performance management				
Clear goals	52.27	10.75	51.95	13.47
Strong monitoring system	29.90	9.97	62.00	26.42
Minimum norms for research performance	34.73	26.82	39.26	26.90
Use of financial rewards	7.70	9.95	16.40	21.93
Use of sanctions	23.91	15.57	24.42	15.33
Main area of research				
Social sciences	0.27	0.45	0.28	0.45
Natural and technical sciences	0.40	0.49	0.37	0.49
Medical and health sciences	0.15	0.36	0.18	0.39
Individual attributes				
Female	0.33	0.47	0.31	0.46
Age	46.11	10.75	47.26	10.43
Associate professor	0.51	0.50	0.50	0.50
Assistant professor/postdoc	0.28	0.45	0.22	0.41
Career expectations				
High hopes for advancement	0.26	0.44	0.27	0.45
Low hopes for advancement	0.42	0.49	0.33	0.47
Work composition				
Average weekly working hours	47.15	8.42	47.38	7.93
Time spend on research (percent)	37.57	20.32	33.47	18.04

2010). This methodology allows for using information for different levels in the same model, thereby making it possible to analyze the relationship between the departments' use of performance management practices the individual researchers' satisfaction with the psychosocial work environment and their perceptions of stress.

We only included researches above Ph.D. level in the analysis (i.e., assistant professor/postdocs, associate professors, and full professors).

Analysis

Overall, university researchers in Denmark are quite satisfied with their psychosocial work environment and experience relative low levels of stress in both 2011 and 2015. There are no significant or substantial changes between the two years. On a scale of 0 to 100 where 100 denote "very satisfied", the mean score for the satisfaction with the psychosocial work environment was 66 in 2011, in 2015 it was 65 (see Table 9.1). Regarding perceptions of stress the mean score was 33 in as well 2011 and 2015. But in both years, there was substantial variation in the individual researchers' perception of the psychosocial work environment and their indicated level of stress (cf. standard deviations in Table 9.1).

Looking instead at the use of performance management practices at university departments, there are clear differences in how much the different instruments are used (see Table 9.1). The top scorers are setting clear organizational goals and the use of performance monitoring systems. While "clear goals" already scored high in 2011, the use of monitoring systems has increased dramatically between 2011 and 2015 and so has the use of financial rewards. However, pecuniary incentives are still the least widespread element of the five in 2015. To some extent, both sanctions and minimum performance standards are used a bit more.

In Tables 9.2 and 9.3, we analyze the relationship between the use of the five included performance management elements and, respectively, the

Table 9.2 Multilevel model predicting satisfaction with the psychosocial work environment (0–100) (standardized coefficients)

	2011		2015	
	Model 1	*Model 2*	*Model 1*	*Model 2*
Performance management				
Clear goals	0.19***	0.19***	0.25***	0.25***
	(0.04)	(0.03)	(0.04)	(0.04)
Strong monitoring system	−0.01	−0.01	0.05	0.04
	(0.09)	(0.07)	(0.04)	(0.04)
Minimum norms for research performance	−0.04	0.00	−0.17***	−0.15**
	(0.04)	(0.03)	(0.04)	(0.05)
Use of financial rewards	0.00	−0.04	−0.04	−0.05
	(0.05)	(0.05)	(0.03)	(0.04)
Use of sanctions	−0.05	−0.05+	−0.07+	−0.05
	(0.03)	(0.03)	(0.04)	(0.04)
Main area of research				
Social sciences		0.08*		−0.04
		(0.04)		(0.04)
Natural and technical sciences		0.05		−0.06
		(0.04)		(0.06)
Medical and health sciences		0.11**		−0.03
		(0.04)		(0.05)
Individual attributes				
Female		−0.11***		−0.08*
		(0.03)		(0.03)
Age		0.03		0.05
		(0.04)		(0.04)

(Continued)

Table 9.2 (Continued)

	2011		2015	
	Model 1	Model 2	Model 1	Model 2
Associate professor		-0.06 (0.05)		-0.02 (0.05)
Assistant professor/ postdoc		-0.06 (0.05)		-0.03 (0.05)
Career expectations				
High hopes for advancement		-0.03 (0.04)		-0.03 (0.04)
Low hopes for advancement		-0.11** (0.04)		-0.15** (0.05)
Work composition				
Average weekly working hours		-0.07** (0.03)		-0.08** (0.03)
Time spend on research (percent)		0.19*** (0.05)		0.19*** (0.04)
Pseudo R^2 (department level)				
Pseudo R^2 (individual level)				
N (departments)	66	66	59	59
N (individuals)	1450	1450	1199	1199

$^+ p < 0.10$, $^* p < 0.05$, $^{**} p < 0.01$, $^{***} p < 0.001$ (standard errors in parentheses)

Table 9.3 Multilevel model predicting stress (0–100) (standardized coefficients)

	2011		2015	
	Model 1	Model 2	Model 1	Model 2
Performance management				
Clear goals	-0.07* (0.03)	-0.06* (0.03)	-0.07+ (0.04)	-0.07* (0.04)
Strong monitoring system	-0.02 (0.08)	-0.03 (0.07)	-0.03 (0.04)	-0.01 (0.04)
Minimum norms for research performance	0.04 (0.03)	0.01 (0.03)	0.06 (0.04)	0.01 (0.05)
Use of financial rewards	-0.01 (0.05)	0.04 (0.05)	-0.03 (0.03)	-0.03 (0.03)
Use of sanctions	-0.01 (0.03)	-0.03 (0.03)	0.02 (0.04)	0.01 (0.04)
Main area of research				
Social sciences		-0.06+ (0.04)		-0.03 (0.04)
Natural and technical sciences		-0.02 (0.03)		-0.01 (0.05)
Medical and health sciences		-0.07* (0.03)		-0.05 (0.04)

	2011		2015	
	Model 1	Model 2	Model 1	Model 2
Individual attributes				
Female		0.05+		0.06+
		(0.03)		(0.03)
Age		−0.09*		−0.06
		(0.04)		(0.04)
Associate professor		0.03		−0.00
		(0.05)		(0.05)
Assistant professor/postdoc		0.04		0.05
		(0.05)		(0.05)
Career expectations				
High hopes for advancement		0.01		0.04
		(0.04)		(0.04)
Low hopes for advancement		0.07+		0.10*
		(0.04)		(0.05)
Work composition				
Average weekly working hours		0.12***		0.22***
		(0.03)		(0.03)
Time spend on research (percent)		−0.23***		−0.20***
		(0.03)		(0.04)
Pseudo R^2 (department level)				
Pseudo R^2 (individual level)				
N (departments)	66	66	59	59
N (individuals)	1450	1450	1199	1199

$^+ p < 0.10$, $^* p < 0.05$, $^{**} p < 0.01$, $^{***} p < 0.001$ (standard errors in parentheses)

nested researchers' satisfaction with the psychosocial work environment and their perceptions of stress. We report the same models for both 2011 and 2015 data. In each case, we estimate two models. Model 1 only enters the independent variables, whereas model 2 includes the control variables.

Satisfaction With the Psychosocial Work Environment

Consistent across the two years, setting clear organizational goals is highly significant and positively associated with the nested researchers' satisfaction with the psychosocial work environment. The higher extent to which the department has clear goals (and strategies for how to reach those goals), the more satisfied the employed researchers on average are.

In 2015, there is a strong, negative relationship between minimum norms for research publication and the researchers' satisfaction with the psychosocial work environment. This is not found for the 2011 data, however. Here, there is no significant association between the use of minimum norms and how the researchers perceive the psychosocial work environment.

Seen across the two years, there are some indications of sanctions potentially being negatively related to how satisfied the researchers are with the psychosocial work environment. In the 2011 data, there is a marginally significant ($p < 0.1$) association between the use of sanctions and satisfaction with the psychosocial work environment in the full model (model 2). In 2015, this is also the case in model 1. However, the negative significant relationship disappears when the control variables are included in model 2.

Regarding the remaining performance management practices (performance monitoring and use of financial rewards), none of these are found to be significantly associated with the researchers' level of satisfaction with the psychosocial work environment in either year.

Table 9.2 also reveals some other interesting things about what relates to the academics' satisfaction with their psychosocial work environment.

In 2011 there are significant differences between the main areas of research. Both Social scientists and researchers within the medical and health sciences are on average more satisfied than their colleagues from the humanities. In 2015 these differences, however, no longer exist.

Women are on average less satisfied than men in 2011 and 2015. There are no significant differences between the different career levels. However, researchers who express low hopes for advancing is generally less satisfied than full professors. Finally, the higher the average number of working hours the researchers' report, the less satisfied they tend to be with their psychosocial work environment. But how the working hours are distributed between different tasks also seems to matter. The more time the researchers have for research relative to other tasks, the more satisfied they on average are with the psychosocial work environment.

Perceptions of Stress

As with satisfaction with the psychosocial work environment, setting clear organizational goals seems to influence the nested researchers' perceptions of stress. The higher extent to which the department has clear goals (and strategies for how to reach those goals), the lower levels of stress the employees on average report in as well 2011 and 2015. However, the association is not as strong as compared to those found regarding the researchers' satisfaction with the psychosocial work environment. It thus indicates a higher level of individual variation between researchers for the same department when it comes to stress.

None of the other analyzed performance management practices is significantly related to the researchers' perceptions of stress.

Looking at the included control variables, we find some of the same patterns as when analyzing the researchers' satisfaction with the psychosocial work environment.

As with regard to the satisfaction with the psychosocial work environment, researchers from the social sciences and the medical and health sciences on average report lower levels of stress than their colleagues from the humanities in 2011. But the relationships are not as strong. As in the earlier analysis, the differences are not found in 2015.

Women tend to feel more stressed than men in 2011 and 2015. The also tended to be less satisfied with the psychosocial work environment (cf. the previous subsection). With regard to stress the relationship in both 2011 and 2015, it is only marginally significant ($p < 0.1$). There are no significant differences between the different career levels. Age is negatively related to higher levels of stress in 2011 but not in 2015. As earlier, career expectations are important: researchers who express low hopes for advancing on average feel more stressed than full professors. Also working hours and work composition is related to the researchers' levels of stress. The higher the average number of working hours the researchers' report, the more stressed they tend to feel. But the higher the percentage of the working hours is spent on research relative to other tasks, the less stressed they on average feel.

Discussion

The intention in performance management is to increase performance by setting clear goals, monitoring performance, and providing incentives (financial rewards and sanctions). Performance management was a part of the managerial reform at Danish universities in 2003 and the underlying principle in the bibliometric system introduced at the universities in 2010. The performance management tools are supposed to work by changing some of the work conditions and the incentive structures in the organizations, so that the employees become more satisfied and committed to their work and thereby raise productivity (Hughes 2005). However, empirical evidence of the employees' reactions to PM is still very sparse and the existing studies show ambiguous results. Even though much of the performance management literature argues for a positive impact of performance management on employees' attitudes and reactions to work, there have also been concerns that using performance tools as a management strategy will help pursue organizational ends, but that this might be at the expense of individual well-being (Fletcher & Williams 1996; Wright 2011; Forrester 2011; Mather & Seifert 2011; Sewel et al. 2012). In this chapter we provide new information by examining two possible but opposing reactions to performance management among the Danish researchers. The analyses focus on how several central performance practices at Danish universities affect the employees' satisfaction with their psychosocial work environment and their perceived levels of stress. The specific mechanisms and processes by which performance management influences university researchers have not been adequately addressed in the literature. Our study therefore provides new insights into some of the conditional mechanisms that seem to be relevant when universities are the setting. The results are furthermore of practical importance for managements of universities in order to secure that the performance management practices as intended improve performance.

Our results showed that researchers at the Danish universities in general had a high satisfaction with their psychosocial work environment and a relatively low level of self-reported stress. This was the case in both 2011 and 2015 and there were no significant changes in the levels of satisfaction and stress over time. This could indicate that the performance management practices had no second-order effect concerning the aggregated levels of satisfaction and stress at the Danish universities. However, there are great variances in the researchers' individual answers and these results therefore do not tell us anything about how the specific performance management tools affect the psychosocial work environment.

If we look at the different management tools over time, we see an interesting tendency. The perception of clear goals among the Danish researchers remains approximately the same from 2011–2015 even though a basic premise underlying performance management is to set up clear goals. It is, however, the management tool that is perceived as the most used of the Danish researchers both in 2011 and 2015. The use of strong monitoring systems, the use of minimum norms for research performance, and the use of financial rewards are all increasing significantly from 2011 to 2015. Thus, these results show a greater awareness among the researchers about these management practices, which indicates that the implementation of these management tools have been a process, which over time have enforced the new management paradigm. Therefore, we should also expect to see stronger effects of these management practice on the researchers' psychosocial work environment in 2015.

If we consider the impact of the performance management practices on the researchers' psychosocial work environment, the results showed that having clear goals increases the researchers' satisfaction with their psychosocial work environment and decreases their perception of stress. This was to be expected. It is generally accepted in this line of research that common and clear goals for the work support greater job satisfaction (Locke & Latham 1990). The research explains the link using the goal-setting theory, which dictates that concrete and well-defined goals may lead to a clearer understanding of the necessary activities for all coworkers and therefore result in better coordination of activities and less redundancy (Konradt et al. 2003: 64). These mechanisms might as well affect the researchers' overall satisfaction with their psychosocial work environment because clear goals clarify what management values as good performance. There is not necessarily a unified agreement among researchers on what constitutes good or bad performance (i.e., research) (e.g., Krejler 2011). However, clear goals from the management may (at least partly) help settle potential conflicts about what constitutes good (or bad) performance at the different university departments. The results also suggest that the effect of clear goals on the researchers' satisfaction with their psychosocial work environment is a bit higher in 2015, indicating that clear goals have become even more important for the employees in 2015. Clear goals also seem to reduce the researchers' perception of stress both in 2011 and 2015. The effect seems to be the same across both years: none of the other examined performance management tools correlates with the researchers' perceptions of stress.

However, in 2015, there is a significant and negative correlation between the use of minimum norms for research performance and the researchers' satisfaction with their psychosocial work environment. This management tool was also the tool that increased the most from 2011–2015 (from a mean on 29.90 to 62.00), and in our data it looks as if this tool actually has an important second-order effect since it reduces the overall satisfaction with the psychosocial work environment. Previous studies have pointed out similar mechanisms. As already mentioned, measuring and monitoring performance also identifies inadequate performers—at least on the performance criteria put forward by the management. Therefore, performance appraisals can be uncomfortable for some employees (Lawler et al. 2012). Sewell et al. (2012) discuss how ambivalent perceptions of performance management often occur among employees who find themselves on the "wrong" end of the scale. These may be employees who meet other tasks or obligations that are not measured in the performance system. In the Danish universities it might be other tasks such as administrative tasks or teaching. Even though such tasks are important at the universities, the performance system makes some employees "win" while others "lose", and therefore the management tool can also be expected to prompt an unhealthy competition resulting in increased suspicion, anxiety, or even stress among the employees (see also Sewell et al. 2012).

Still, if we consider the results all together, an overall conclusion must be that the performance management practices do not seem to affect the researchers' psychosocial work environment to a high degree, since there are no significant changes at the aggregated level across time and since only minimum norms for research as a management tool seem to correlate negatively with satisfaction with the psychosocial work environment.

If we look at the control variable, we also see some interesting tendencies over time. In 2011 the researchers from medical and health science were more satisfied with their psychosocial work environment than their colleagues within humanities research. The same goes for stress. In 2011 the researchers in social science and medical and health science perceived less stress than their colleagues in humanities research. However, these differences disappear over time, since there are no significant differences between the researchers' satisfaction with their psychosocial work environment and their perception of stress between the main areas of research in 2015. We cannot rule out that these differences are related to differences in general work environment issues across the areas, but if we interpret these result as a consequence of the reform and not least as a consequence of the introduction of the bibliometric system at the Danish universities in 2010, the lower levels of satisfaction and higher levels of stress in 2011 among the researchers in the humanities research might relate to the fact that the humanities researchers were facing the biggest changes in their performance management practices in comparison with for example social science and medical and health science, which were used to the use of financial rewards and a publication pattern that resembled the publication expectations in the bibliometric system. From the psychosocial work environment research on employees' reactions to organizational changes, we know that this is an expected pattern. Very often employees react with frustration and stress to organizational changes in the beginning of the implementation period, while these negative or sometimes ambivalent reactions often disappear over time when the new practices has been fully integrated in the daily organizational routines (for example Carnall 2003; Piederit 2000). These results indicate that it has been a bigger change in the humanities (see also Mouritzen & Opstrup 2019), and that the researchers in these research areas therefore have reacted with negative affective responses in the beginning of the implementation period, but that these negative responses have dampened over time.

We also see a pattern across time that the female researchers are less satisfied and perceive more stress than their male colleagues. However, we cannot relate these results to the new management practices, since they do not change significantly over time, and because they probably describe a tendency at the universities related to more general gender equality issues. The same goes for the researchers' career expectations. We see a general pattern across time that the researchers with low hopes for advancement are less satisfied and perceive more stress than their colleagues. These results are probably related to the high competition for advancements in the universities and not to the new management practices.

However, if we look at the researchers' work composition, we see some interesting results. The descriptive comparison between 2011 and 2015 showed that on average the researcher spent significantly less time on research (compared to other tasks) in 2015 than in 2011. At the same time our results showed that the more time the researchers spend on research, the more satisfied they were and the less stress they perceived in both 2011 and 2015. We do not argue that it is the performance management system that causes this reduction in time spend on research among the researchers. However, in the performance management system at the Danish universities (especially in the bibliometric system) it is primarily research performance that the researchers are measured and monitored on. Therefore, it could be expected that it would cause frustration among the researchers if they do not have enough time to do research. Even though we do not see big differences in the correlation effects over time in our study, it is an issue that the managers should be aware of to secure a good psychosocial work environment in the future.

There are of course limitations to this study that should be mentioned. First of all, the method presupposes a one-way causal direction from the element of the performance management practices to the researchers' perception of their psychosocial work environment and their stress levels. Even though we do have data across time, we analyze the data as two cross-sectional datasets, and thereby we are not able to determine the causal directions of the mechanisms. It is also important to be aware that the employees' perceptions of their work conditions and their related satisfaction and stress levels are likely to be reciprocal over time. Although we partly avoided this problem using a multilevel analysis strategy, the current conclusions could profit from research in future longitudinal or experimental studies in order to develop a more comprehensive understanding of the complex causal relation between performance management practices and psychosocial work environment. Moreover, using aggregated department means ignores potential important variation within department between, e.g., different groups, units etc. More truly objective measures would be preferable. It would also have been interesting to include a measure of the individual researcher's performance. But how this measure should be constructed and included is highly debatable. Finally, even though this study points to broader theoretical and practical implications, the study reflects a particular regional reality at the Danish universities and the specific results should therefore only be directly generalized to other contexts with great caution. To expand further on our understanding of how performance management actually functions as a management strategy, the next step would be to compare the results from this study to similar studies in other countries and in other professions.

Note

1. We cannot asses to which extent minimum norms are formal rules or informal norms.

Reference

Wulandari, P., Mangundjaya, W. & Utoyo D.B. 2015, "Is Job Satisfaction a Moderator or Mediator on the Relationship Between Change Leadership and Commitment to Change?", in *Contemporary Issues in Management and Social Science Research*, eds. D. Wickramasinghe, A.F.A. Hamid & K. Pirzada, pp. 104–111.

10 Conclusion

Niels Ejersbo, Carsten Greve,
and Signe Pihl-Thingvad

Universities are caught in the middle of some profound transformations in this age. There is a transformation in the way they are governed; a transformation in the way academic performance is measured, evaluated, and controlled; a transformation in how university employees are exposed to stress symptoms; and a transformation in the way universities are managed.

The "Humboldt-type university" or the "Republic of Science" (Polanyi 1962) has been under siege for several decades now, and it is highly unlikely that the universities will return to those older organizational forms after the transformations and the reforms that have washed over universities worldwide.

In this book we have addressed many of the issues from a particular empirical dataset that we were able to gather in Denmark in a specific period of time. The extensive dataset has allowed us to take a fresh look at where the universities currently stand in the transformative period mentioned above. Now that we have reached the end of the book, what might we possibly conclude on some of the overall findings reported in the individual chapters?

Our argument will be that universities may have left the secure quarters of the "Republic of Science", but they have not arrived at a safe haven yet where universities' place in the construct of society is secure and settled. Some higher education scholars and organizational scholars have argued that universities have strived to become "complete" organizations, but we argue that they are not there yet, and are, in fact, still in a transformative phase. What it does mean is that universities in Western Europe and specifically in a Nordic country like Denmark have become "normal" public sector organizations with all that it entails. Universities have become "normalized" as public sector organizations.

Following on from that argument, our second argument is that the NPM influenced universities in many, important ways, but that universities have also responded to other governance trends in a layered approach, so universities today are expected to be aligning themselves with partners both in other universities and in the private sector in order to build alliances or partnerships. At the same, the consequence of the performance management regime inherent in the NPM reforms has been that the state has maintained or regained control over the universities to the extent that universities may fit what some researchers have described as the "whole-of-government" or "Neo-Weberian State". In the book we show how performance management and contracts have been deployed to see continuing control over universities by the state, and how performance management in the form of bibliometric performance systems have been implemented for university departments and their researchers. Universities are under the control of the state despite the rhetoric of NPM to promote liberation management (Light 2006) and the decentralization of management responsibility.

The third part of our argument is that there are consequences of these findings for research on universities. Instead of treating universities as something special, future studies should concentrate on comparing universities with other forms of organizations that deliver public service. Universities then join the health sector in "not being so special anymore", which then opens up opportunities for comparing the organization and management of universities, hospitals, police stations, fire departments, social services organizations, and many other types of organizations. The normalization or isomorphism of the form of the public service organization allows for new cross-organizational comparisons that can benefit both the study of universities and also the field of organization theory for public service organizations.

Neither Organized Anarchies, Nor Complete Organizations: Transformations Led to the Normalization of Universities as Organizations Delivering a Public Service

Universities have long been regarded as something special: either as organized anarchies in the memorable phrase of Michael Cohen and James March (Cohen & March 1974) and their colleagues, or as striving to become "complete organizations" in the sense the Swedish organizational researcher Nils Brunsson (2013) described in organization theory literature. The transformation began in earnest with the introduction of NPM and its related emphasis on management and markets: Organizations should be modelled on private sector companies, or at least get inspired by them, and they should abandon the "clan" system that Ouchi talked about, and the slow and ineffective administration that was associated with the collegiate system. The rise of NPM led to the label of "the enterprise university" (Marginson & Considine 2000) which served as the new model for the modern university. But as much of the research agenda in higher education studies and the organization of universities have shown, there have been a number of problems with implementing

NPM. The problems come from the professionalization aspects, as university employees do not like to be told what to do and do have strong academic norms guiding them. University employees like to develop their own research agenda according to their interest and quest for new knowledge, Universities were often disorganized systems that did not lend itself easily to the quick fixes of the consultants' preferences that became associated with the practical side of NPM. So NPM was met with resistance in the university sector.

The transformations occurred anyway, and the universities did move towards the model called "the enterprise university". However, our point here is that the transformation is still ongoing. Universities may have left the Humboldtian ideas behind, and universities may have adopted a number of NPM tools along the way, but the transformation to a "complete" organizations with firm leadership, clear division of labor, and clear organizational structure in a transparent format recognizable to all, have not occurred.

Therefore, we argue that our book shows how universities have not become just like any type of private sector organizations, and that universities still possess a number of distinct qualities and marking. Universities can perhaps more accurately be characterized as being "normal public service organizations"; they are "normalized" in the sense that they now look more or less like any organization delivering a public service in a Western European country like Denmark. This means that they are neither an "old public administration" bureaucracy and hierarchy; nor do they assume the "clan" or "Republic of Science" character of old, and yet they are not in any sense complete as organizations. Instead they assume many of the same characteristics as other similar type of organizations, like hospitals and the police, that deliver services to the public. They struggle with an organizational structure that both sees them as a decentralized organization, yet still an integral part of the state. People try to become CEOs or "presidents", yet they still have to respond to initiatives inside the governance structure of the state, and under the influence of the minister of research and higher education.

The "normalization" of the universities into more common (if we may) public sector organizations can be seen clearly in the empirical analysis of our data set. Performance contracts were introduced, and they were first billed as being about "liberation management" and supporting performance management known within NPM. Yet the empirical research shows that control has maintained, if not increased, since the university reform of 2003, and performance contracts are now wired into how the government governs the universities. We see that too with the introduction of university boards. The boards were supposed to resemble boards in private sector companies in many ways, and important people were appointed to the board. The board has become an intermediate institution between the president/CEO and the state. Our empirical research shows that board members had different perspectives on what their roles were. Some board members concentrated on focusing on the budget and on the strategy, while other board members assumed that they were asked to serve at their old university as a kind of show of commitment to the university ideals that they were supposed to guard. The key figures in the board, the chairpersons of the board, also expressed views that the government was controlling the boards and the universities too tightly, and that the board structure and board governance did not resemble the experience some of them had from the private sector. In other words, the institution of the board in the larger institution of the new university is unclear to a large degree. Even attempts to make corrections and be more specific in formulating the role of the boards on behalf of the ministry does not seem to have eliminated the imprecise status of the boards to this day. These uncertainties are, however, not unlike what we see in the health sector, in the police, or in the transport sector where public service organizations are muddling through. Layers upon layers of administrative regulations and governance mechanisms are being loaded onto the public sector organizations (with occasional initiatives from governments to "cut red tape" or "deregulate" activities). Universities are becoming "normal", and, like any other public service organization, they have to fight a number of competing demands and expectations at the same time their budgets are being cut, and all the while they are supposed to be able to create public value (Bovaird & Loeffler eds. 2015; Moore 2013; Van der Wal 2017).

Continuing Governance by the State Over Universities Despite New Public Management Reforms

The big lure of NPM was always that public organizations would be set free, manage their own affairs, and compete in a marketplace for customers and resources (in the case of universities, this meant compete for students and research funding). Performance management was placed in the center of NPM, and the reliance on performance contracts meant that the performance targets would be specified for the universities right down to the individual department and then implicitly to the individual researcher. With the advent of the use of bibliometric data to trace the research activities of the individual researcher, it became possible in principle to measure the individual performance of the single researcher, and thereby to evaluate progress or the lack thereof. At the same time, the performance management focus meant that there was risk of a more stressful working environment at the universities.

As we have seen, the NPM reforms have not been implemented to the largest extent, and universities have not become "complete organizations" in the sense of having full autonomy and decision-making power of their resources, and neither are their organization charts sheltered from interventions by the government. The empirical results we have presented in this book suggest that the governance of universities is ongoing by the state, and that the NPM-inspired reforms of performance management have not had the desired effect of turning the Danish universities into "enterprise universities".

The board is supposed to be securing the role of the university as a separate, performance-oriented organization. Our research shows that board members have different perspectives on what their roles are. Some board members see the role as being guardian of the university organization, and protecting it from unnecessary government interference. Other board members see their role as serving both the state and the university by focusing solely on the budget and on broad performance targets. Some board members think that their roles are to support the President (CEO) in what he or she is doing. And then there are board members who are wanting to give something back to their old university, and they do not have strong preferences of what their precise mission on the board is.

Performance management contracts were supposed to be a part of a "liberation management" move towards setting the university free and turning it towards a "complete organization". But the performance contracts became a vehicle for the state to still press for demands regarding the universities. Even though there were different perceptions of the contracts among the board members, they used the contracts in their managerial work and decisions. An interesting picture appeared when analyzing the content in the contract. Around 2012, input and process measures increased while output and outcome measures decreased. This in- and decrease were independent of any formal alterations to the government model. This suggests that a more indirect reregulation was introduced in the form of layering more micromanagement tools in the contracts, which, despite a continuing formal autonomy, lowered the real managerial autonomy at the universities. Hence the type of control that the state practiced towards universities may have changed in character because of the performance contracts, but the control did not disappear. Performance contracts still tied the universities to the state, and the governance of universities by the state is still intact.

Use of bibliometric data was supposed to make it easier to use monetary rewards towards researchers as suggested by the principal-agent model in organizational economics theory. The empirical results show that monetary rewards have been allocated for specific performances by researchers. However, many of the researchers in the empirical material were ignorant of the possibilities of getting rewarded by the universities for their performance. The analysis showed that minimum norms for publication did not have a significant effect on the ignorance of the performance system. Also, the allocation of economic rewards for publication did not have an effect of the level of ignorance either. The only factor that did seem to matter was a strong monitoring system of researchers, which did have some effect on the level of ignorance. As was stated in Chapter 9, the principal-agent version of the performance management theory supposes that selfish agents will know about the performance management system and try to circumvent it or game it in a strategic manner, but our empirical results from the Danish universities suggest that it is not the case in real-life universities.

How did the performance management reforms have an effect on the working conditions for university researchers, and did it lead to stress symptoms? We focused on this by looking at the nested researchers' satisfaction with the psychosocial work environment and their perceptions of stress. Overall the university researchers were quite satisfied with their psychosocial work environment and experienced a relatively low level of stress in both 2011 and 2015 and there were no significant changes over time. Thus, the performance management tools did not seem to reshape the overall perceptions of their work environment. In other words, it did not create a situation where second-order effects of performance management appeared. However, the results indicated that the researchers may have become more aware of the new performance management tools over time (from 2011 to 2015). The question that remains is whether the new governance structure and its inherent performance management tools have cascaded down through the organizations in the Danish universities in a way that actually impacts on the researchers' daily work routines. The data only show small signs of this. Still, whether this means that the performance management tools have just started to have an impact on the researchers' work and that we do not really see the effects yet, or that this is the only (and rather small) effect that the reforms have had on the researchers' work environment is hard to determine. Within the current data (covering only a certain period of time from 2011 to 2015) it seems as if the major managerial changes might be found at the higher hierarchical levels of the organization. This might be the reason why the researchers' psychosocial work environment seems relatively unaffected.

Summing up, the empirical results do not point to a total commitment to the performance management regime suggested by principal-agent theory and NPM reforms in general. Universities have not become fully independent of the state, and they are not organizations that compete freely on a market for students and resources. The introduction of performance contracts did not lead to an absence of control. Instead, we can say that there is continuing governance and control by the state over universities in Denmark.

The Implications of Our Findings for the Future Study of University Governance

Finally, we would like to address what our findings mean for how university governance can be studied in the future. Of course, there are many aspects of university governance that still needs to be explored, and there will be ample opportunities to pursue even more studies of the performance of universities as the methodologies in the field of Public Administrations continues to get more sophisticated.

As indicated in our previous discussion, perhaps a key finding is that although there is merit to the specialization of studying sectors by themselves (and we recognize that higher education studies is such a field of research), it seems that the need to compare universities with other kinds of organizations can be a potential fruitful avenue of research in the future. Universities seem to have lost that special ingredient that sets them apart from all other types of organizations delivering public services. Of course, the universities have many peculiar characteristics, including advanced knowledge production, but universities are now struggling with many of the same issues as many other types of public service organizations: How to structure the relationship between politicians and bureaucrats? How to design a governance structure that includes intermediate bodies like a board of directors? How to balance the pressure from market forces with the pressure to forming alliances and partnerships to the pressure of delivering concrete public value that satisfy both the political overseers and the end-users? How to balance the need for using performance management systems with the need for securing tolerable working conditions that do not create stress? How to deal with the exposure to the media while maintaining a core corporate culture? How to relate to demands from users and customers who aspire to be cocreators or coproducers while at the same time formulating and implementing long-term business strategies? How to present a business model for the organization that will adhere to the wishes of the politicians (that often approve budgets), and comply with the aspirations of the managers, employees, and stakeholders related to the organization?

Designing comparative analyses that contrast the perspective from universities with perspectives from hospitals or the police could have the potential to advance the wider work of a theory of how public service organizations operate. Many Public Administration and Public Management scholars are already engaged in these activities, and it would be beneficial to study university governance with other types of public service organizations in the future.

References

Bovaird, T. & Loeffler, E. 2015, *Public Management and Governance*, Routledge, London.

Brunsson, N. 2013, "New Public Organisations: A Revivalist Movement", in *The Ashgate Research Companion to New Public Management*, eds. T. Christensen & P. Lægreid, Ashgate, Aldershot.

Cohen, M.D. & March, J.G. 1974, *Leadership and Ambiguity: The American College President*, Carnegie Commission on Higher Education, New York.

Light, P.C. 2006, "The Tides of Reforms Revisited. Patterns in Making Government Work 1945–2002". *Public Administration Review*, vol. 66, no. 1, pp. 6–19.

Marginson, S. & Considine, M. 2000, *The Enterprise University: Power, Governance and Reinvention in Australia*, Cambridge University Press, Cambridge.

Moore, M. 2013, *Recognizing Public Value*, Harvard University Press, Cambridge, MA.

Polanyi, M. 1962, "The Republic of Science: Its Political, and Economic Theory", *Minerva*, vol. 1, no. 1.

Van der Wal, Z. 2017, *The 21st Century Public Manager*, Palgrave MacMillan, London.

Index

Note: Page numbers in *italic* indicate a figure and page numbers in **bold** indicate a table on the corresponding page.

Aarhus University 23
academia 7, 25, 34, 83, 119; modern management and working conditions 140–157
academic tribes 4, 69
administrative system 28
agency problems 118
Amaral, A. 84
Ammons, D.N. & Roenigk, D.J. 142
Andersen, Lotte Bøgh 7
audit society 81
Australia 32

bad performer 63
Becher, T. 6
Berry, F. 123
bibliometric data 162
Bibliometric Research Indicator 32
bibliometric system 153, 156
bivariate "effect" 134
Blaschke, S. 85
BNP 31, 34
board governance model 109
Bouckaert, G. 8, 28, 29, 44, 70, 82
Boyne, G.A. 142
Bozeman, B. 84
Brewer, G.A. 142
Brunsson, N. 3, 4, 159
Bryson, J.M. 3, 83, 96
bureaucratic mode of interaction 69
bureaucratic organization 69

Capano, G. 44, 100, 101, 107, 109, 113, 114; typology 100
causal model *126*
causal relationship 127

Challenging the Performance Movement 8
chance events 28
Cheng, S. 84
Christensen, T. 35, 103, 104
civil servants 60–62
Clinton/Gore reform 28
Cohen, Michael 159
competency trap 45
complete organizations 5
constitutive effects 63
Copenhagen Business School (CBS) 20
Copenhagen Psychosocial Questionnaire (COPSOQ) 146
Crosby, B. 83, 96

Dahler-Larsen, P. 63
Danish primary schools 42
Danish setting labor unions 120
Danish stipend program 32
Danish universities 18, 30, 31, 35, 38, 41, 45, 50, 52, 61, 88, 91, 98; analyses 106–107, 131–135; autonomy and performance management at 102–105; data and measurements 105–106; design and data 127; hypotheses 125–127; incentive systems at 120; management model 107–110; measurement 128–131; ministry's steering of 107–110; performance contracts 110–113; steering-at-a-distance 101–102
Danish University Act 44; and ministerial orders 26

Danish University Law 88
data: departments in study, sampling
   20; desk research 25–26;
   interviews 24–25; overview **19–20**;
   questionnaire surveys 21–24
de Boer, H. 44
DEG 2
Degn, L. 44
department chairs: challenges for
   94–95; data, methods, and measures
   86–88; leadership and management
   roles 90–92; public managers, public
   governance 81–83; strategy 92–94;
   universities, management focus
   83–86
DeSeve, E. 29
desk research 25–26
development contracts 25, 51, 111
disaggregation + competition +
   incentivatization 2
DKK 32, 33
Dunleavy, P. 2
dynamic inertia 30

economic development 38
elite decision-making 28
Elo, A-L. 146
Enders, J. 104
enterprise university 4, 160
EU-funded projects 31
EU Horizon 2020 program 33
executive committee 84
expectancy theory 119
exploratory factor analysis 71, 86
extrinsic motivation 119

faculty members 122
Ferlie, E. 84
Fording, R. 114
formal hierarchy 6
formal leadership training 89
four rule types **48–49**, 50
Fremdriftsreformen 33, 36
Frølich, N. 85
Frost, J.J.F. 85
funnel of causality 125

Ginsberg, B. 84
globalization strategy 33
"Governance, Funding and
   Performance of Universities"
   project 19, 51
governance reforms 40
Government Act *see* University Act

Governmental and University Acts,
   1989 and 2015 47
governmental control 41–42
governmental control, autonomous
   university: delegating authority
   and stating requirements 56–57;
   performance and production rules
   58–59; regulating from a distance
   51–55; self-governing universities
   55–57
governmental regulation of Danish
   universities, 1989 to 2015 40–64;
   governmental control, autonomous
   university 51–59; methodological
   approach 45–51; performance
   management 42–43; reforms
   43–44; rule development dynamics
   59–61; rules 44–45; university
   autonomy and governmental
   control 41–42

Halligan, J. 8, 70
hierarchical conflicts 95
hierarchical mode governance 101
hierarchical organizational structure 4
higher education: management
   revolution 84; steering and
   autonomy in 100–101
Humboldtian organizational culture
   141
Humboldtian tradition 114
Humboldt model 1, 7, 103
Humboldt-type university 158

ignorance level 134, 135
incentives schemes 118
incentive systems 120, 122–125
Innovation Fund Denmark 33
institutional decision-making 6
internal hierarchy, establishment 5–6
international reform movement 5

Jakobsen, M.L.F. 42, 47, 55

Kamensky, J.M. 28
Kettl, Donald 8
Klijn, E.H. 83
Konsistorium 6, 30
Koppenjan, J. 83
Korunka, C. 145

leader-identity 96
leadership: attention 131; and
   management 6–7

"Leadership for the common good in shared-power world" 83
loosely coupled systems 4
Luetjens, J. 28

management: hegemony theory 68; and leadership 6–7; reactions 76; revolution 83; tools 99, 154, 155
managerialism 4, 7
managerial professional model 7
managers, department chairs 88–90
March, James 69, 159
micromanagement 99, 109
Mintrom, M. 28
mixed methods approach 18
modern governance reforms 40
modern managers 76, 81–96
monetary rewards 124
Moore, Mark 3, 7, 29
Mortensen, P.B. 42, 47, 55
Moynihan, D.P. 42, 62, 64, 113, 123, 142
Multi-Level Governance in Universities 85

"Neo elements" 44
Neo-Weberian State (NWS) model 2, 36, 44, 82, 96; manager 83
New Public Governance (NPG) paradigm 2, 34, 82, 96; manager 83
New Public Management (NPM) models 2–4, 6–8, 37, 81, 82, 85, 86, 91, 93, 95, 101, 118, 140, 145, 158–163; managers 82
Noblet, A.J. 145
non-causal association, academic field 126
non-tenured faculty 136
Norway 32
Nvivo 25

official reform proposals 27
old administrators 81–96
Olsen, J.P. 44
one-time bonuses 122
online survey program 23
organizational autonomy 98, 115
organizational economics theory 162
organization structures, formalizing 5–6
organized anarchies 4

Park, S. 123
Patashnik, E.M. 29
penetrated hierarchies 1

performance-based university research funding system 32, 118
performance contracts 5, 30, 100, 108–113, 160; contents in 111–113; use of contracts 110–111
performance doctrine 8–9
performance indicators 99
performance information systems 43
performance management (PM) 42–43, 70, 98, 140; analysis 148–153; contracts 162; control variables 147; data and measurement 145–148; dependent variables 146; estimation, data 147–148; independent variables 146–147; mode of interaction 73, 78; movement 8; normative doctrine of 42; partial adoption of 43; psychosocial work environment, satisfaction 151–152; and psychosocial working conditions 143–145; in public sector 142–143; stress perceptions 152–153; systems 4
performance management reforms 163; partial adoption of 62–64
performance monitoring 147
performance rules 42
policy instrument 41
political agreement 30
political system 28
Pollitt, C. 7, 28–29, 44, 82, 142, 145
Power, Michael 81
power index 84
procedural mode governance 101
production rules 42
professional autonomy 101, 103
psychosocial work environment 154, 155
publication command systems 118
publicly funded resources 60
public management reform theories 28–29
public managers 114; paradigms, public governance 81–83
public organizations 69
public sector institutions 67
public sector leadership 7
public sector management 8, 81
public sector reforms 3

qualification bonuses 147
qualitative comparative fuzzy-set analysis (fsQCA) 123
questionnaire surveys 21–24

Radin, B.A. 8, 28
real organizations 70, 92
recruitment rules 62
rectors 7
reforms: entrepreneur 38; in the
  public sector and universities 2–5
regulation 41, 42; regulating from a
  distance 51–55
reinforcement theory 119
Republic of Science 158, 160
"Retsinformation" 46
reward certainty 122
rewards 119
Roskilde University (RUC) 20
Rourke, F.E. and Brookes, G.E. 84
Røvik, K.A. 123
rubber stamp thesis 68
rules delegating authority 49
rules stating requirements 50

Sahlin-Andersson, K. 3
Salter, B. and Tapper, T. 85
Schram, S.F. 114
Schulz, M. 69
second-order effects 143
Seeber, M. 4, 7
self-governance 52; mode governance
  101
Sewell, G. 155
Siegrist, J. 144
slicing strategies 119
socioeconomic context 28
sociological institutionalism 123
Sørensen, M. 44
Soss, J. 114
Sporn, B. 84
stakeholders 45
steering-at-a-distance mode
  governance 101–102
steering-from-a-distance model 112
Streeck, W. 27
stress 146; perceptions 152–153
strong monitoring systems 134

Technical University of Denmark
  (DTU) 20, 23
Thelen, K. 27
theoretical reform model 29
traditional university systems 104

"Universitetsevaluering.
  Evalueringsrapport 2009" 31
universities, management focus:
  better management 83–84;
  management and control 84–85;
  management and governance,
  literature 86; New Public
  Governance type 85–86
universities in Denmark, reform
  pattern 33–37
University Act (Styrelsesloven) 30,
  44, 46, 49–54, 61, 88, 96, 99; and
  ministerial orders 41, 45, 46
university autonomy 41–42
university governance 1, 18, 31, 106,
  163–164; reforms 30–33, 36
university management: board
  influence and interaction modes
  68–70; board influence and
  management interaction 73–78;
  data, method, and measures
  70–72
university managers 62
university reforms 6

Van Dooren, W. 8, 113
Veblen, Thorstein 83
Vedung, E. 42, 49
Velux Foundation 19, 51

Walker, R.M. 142
web-based questionnaires 21, 70
Weber, M. 82
Weberian elements 44
West, Darrell 1

Zhou, H.K. 69

Printed in the United States
by Baker & Taylor Publisher Services